# This Book
## IS
## THE PROPERTY OF

_____

_____

_____

_____

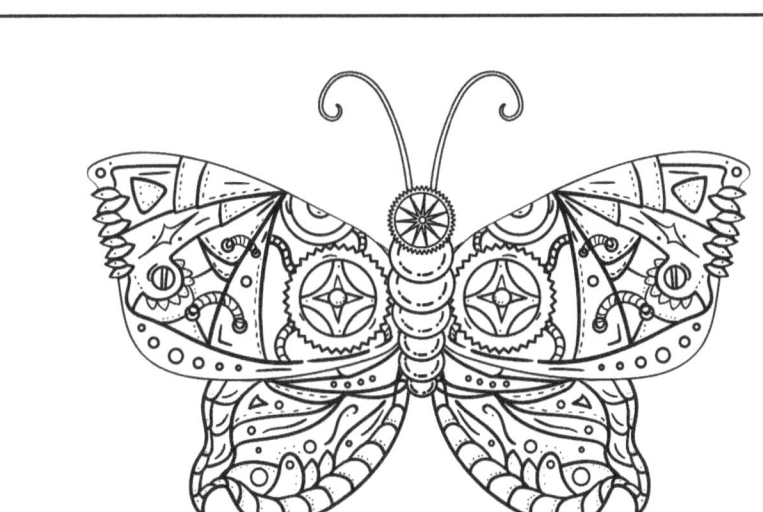

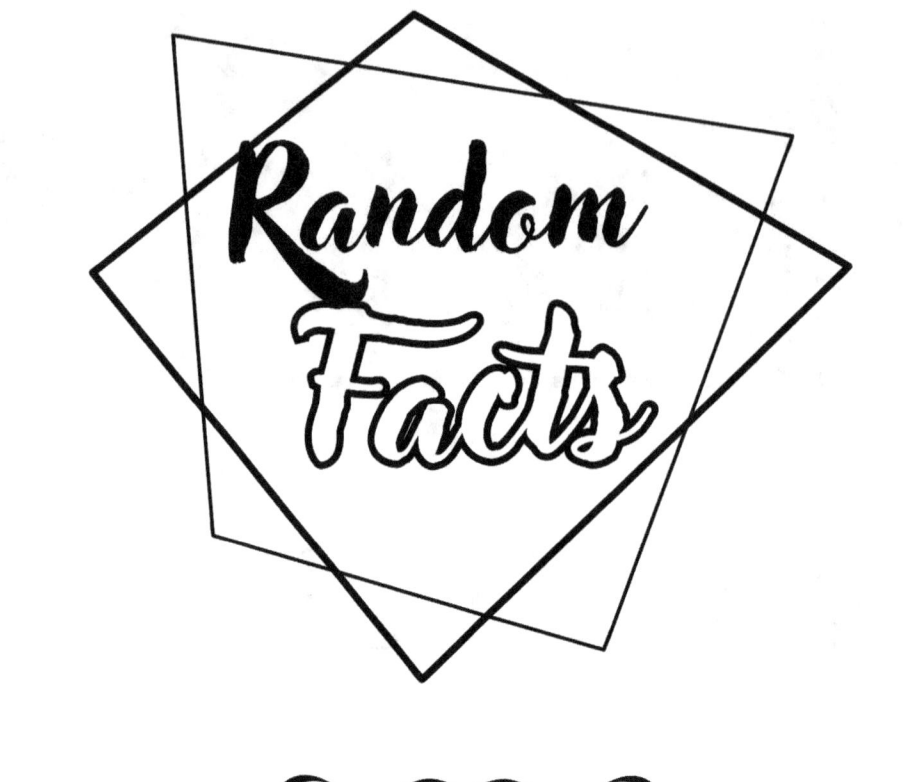

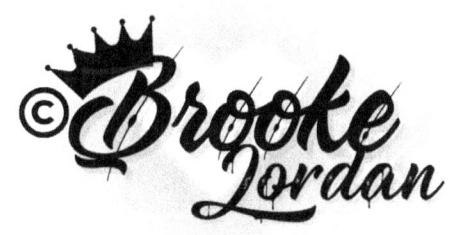

<u>Primary</u> Author Page

# AMAZON.COM/AUTHOR/BJOS_JOURNALS_ETC

<u>Secondary</u> Author Page

# AMAZON.COM/AUTHOR/BROOKEBJOJORDAN

Etsy Shop

# XOBJOS.ETSY.COM/

*Thank You*

*xoxo b.jo*

Feel free to send any feedback or comments to
xo.bjo.ox@gmail.com

Out My Way Yo Cause I'm that BITCH Who Really Dont Play-Doh

# About the Artist

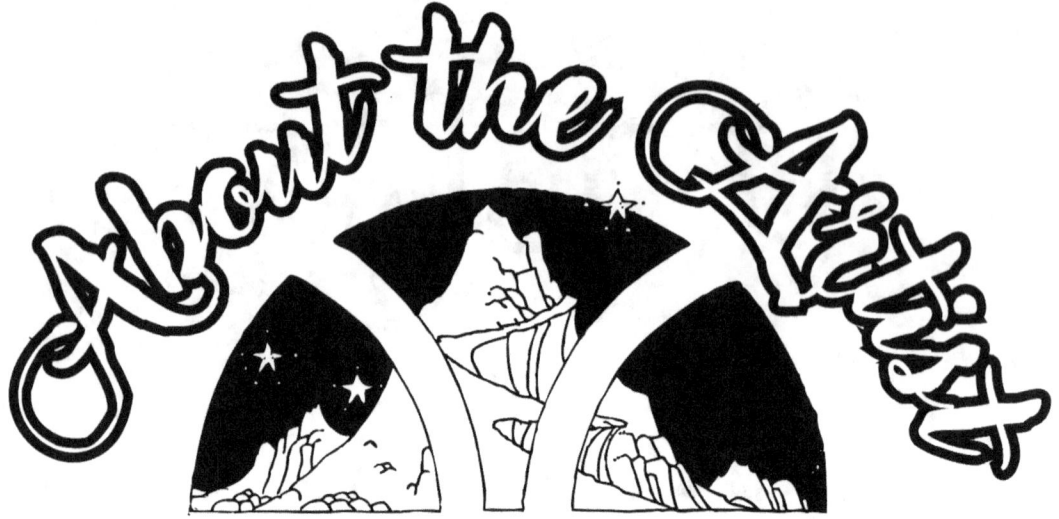

| Colored by | |
|---|---|
| On this day | |
| Notes | |

XOBJos.Etsy.com

Brooke Jordan

Amazon.com/author/bjos_Journals_etc

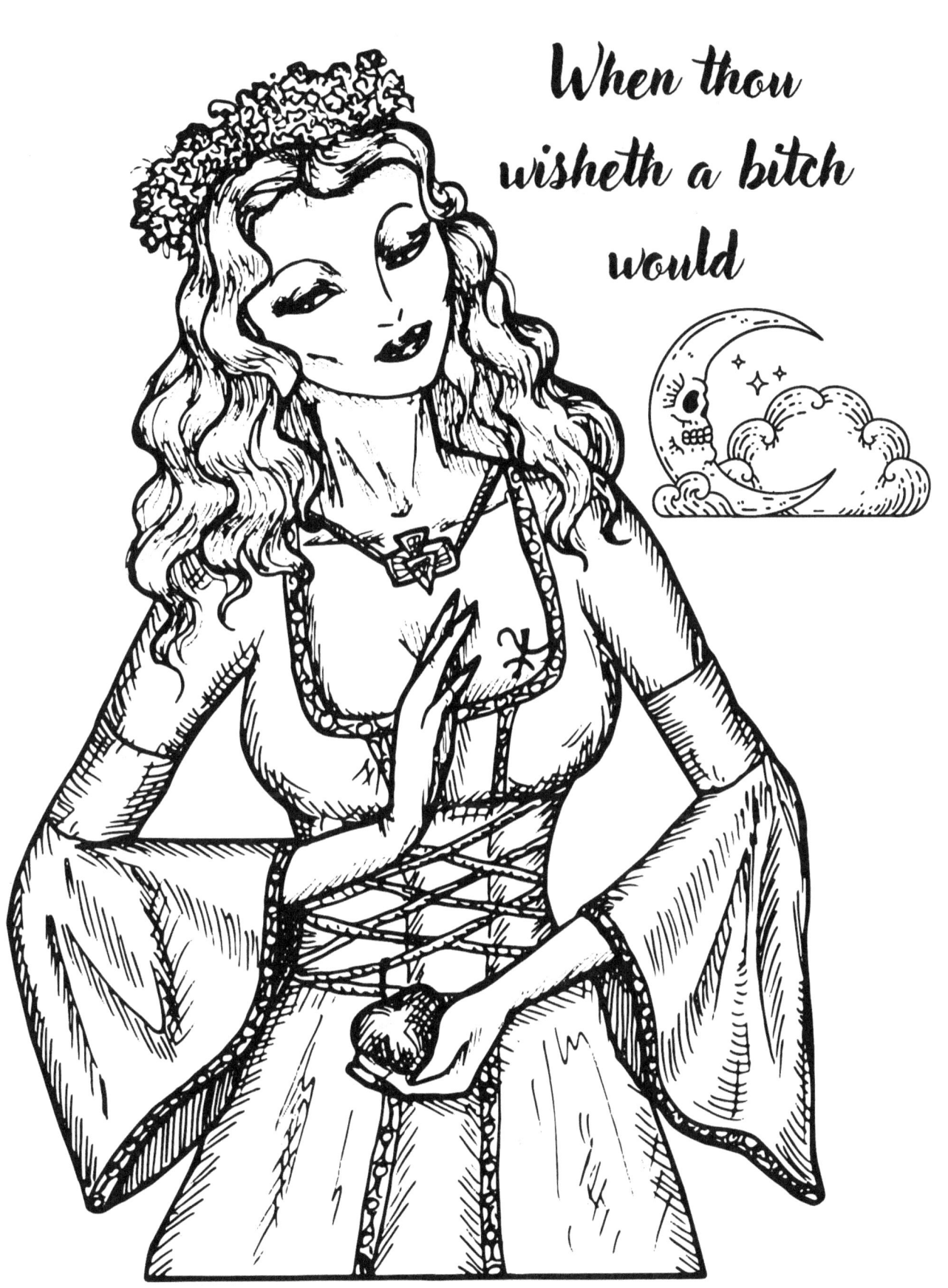

# About the Artist

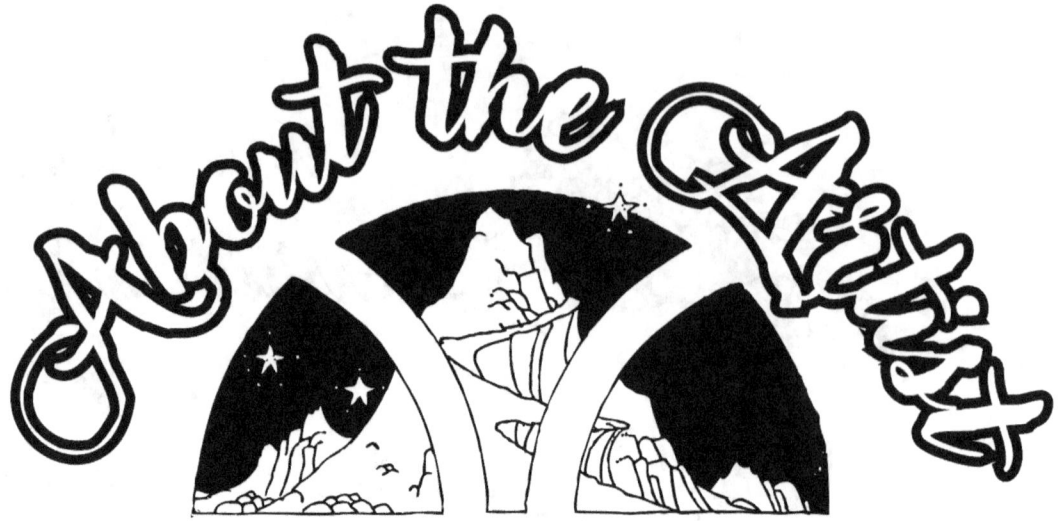

| Colored by | |
|---|---|
| On this day | |
| Notes | |

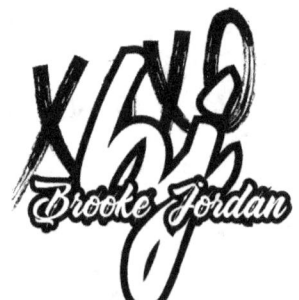

Amazon.com/author/bjos_Journals_etc

# Just The Tip Promise

## What? It'll only hurt for a minute.

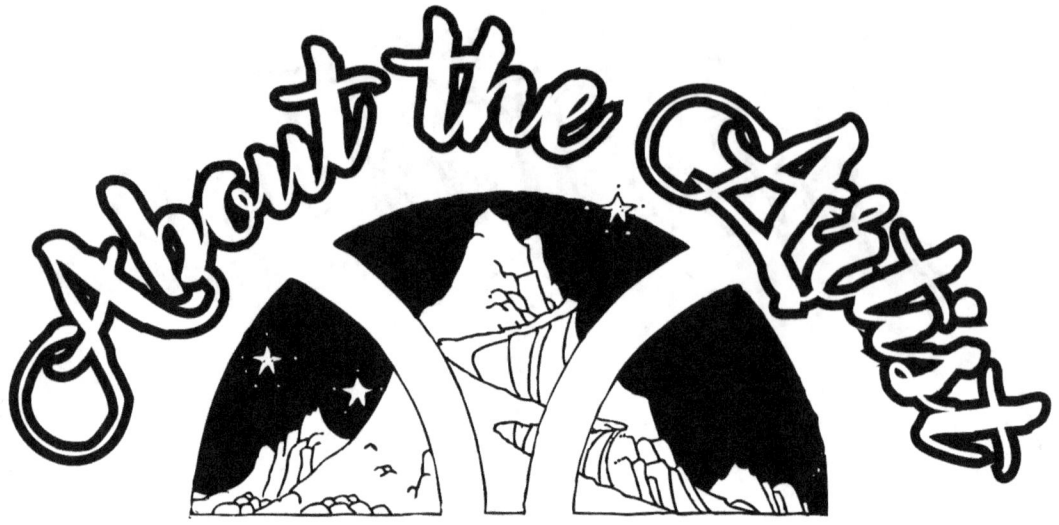

# About the Artist

| Colored by | |
|---|---|
| On this day | |
| Notes | |

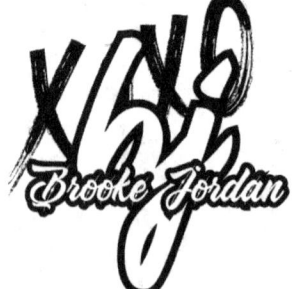

Amazon.com/author/bjos_Journals_etc

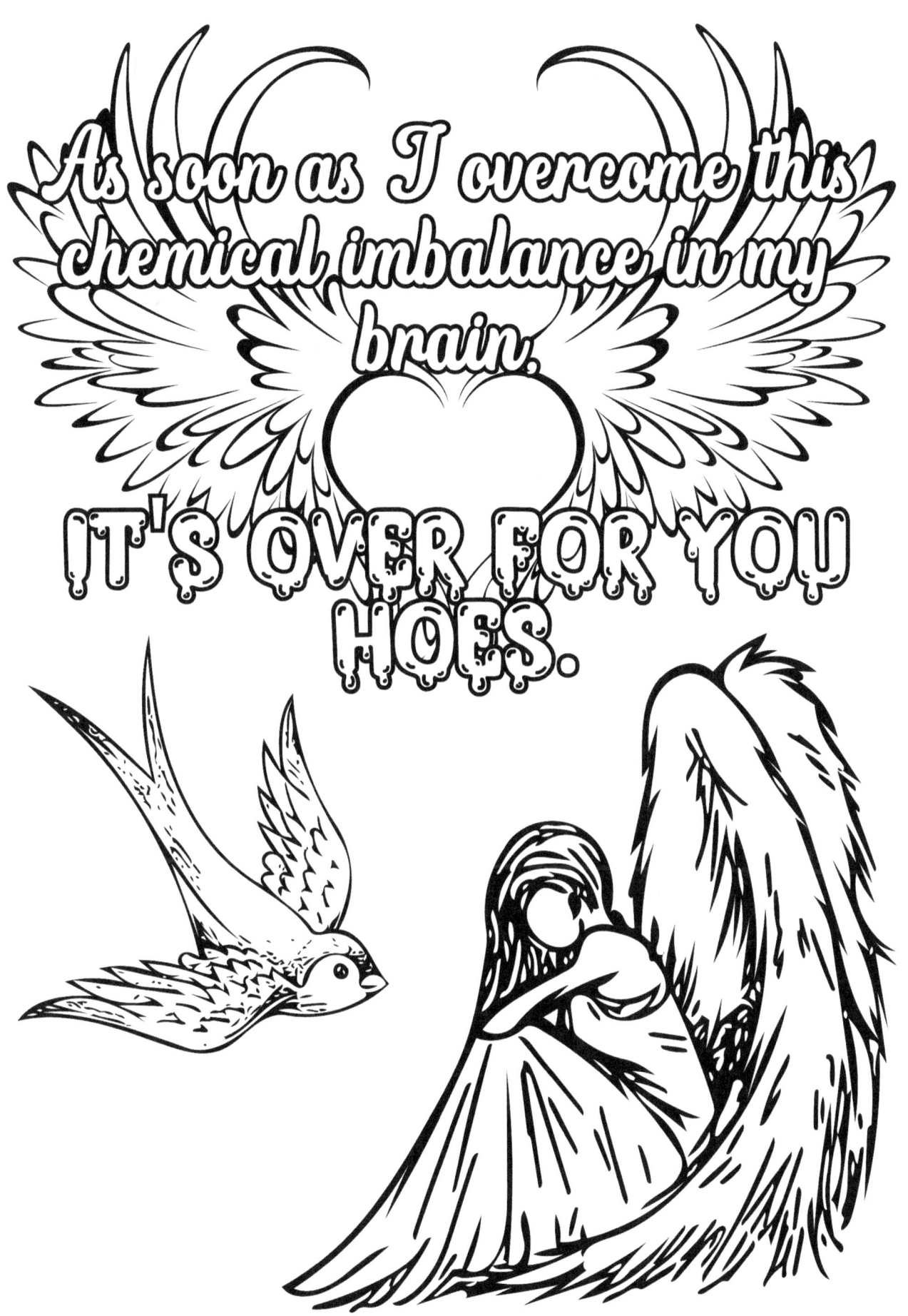

# About the Artist

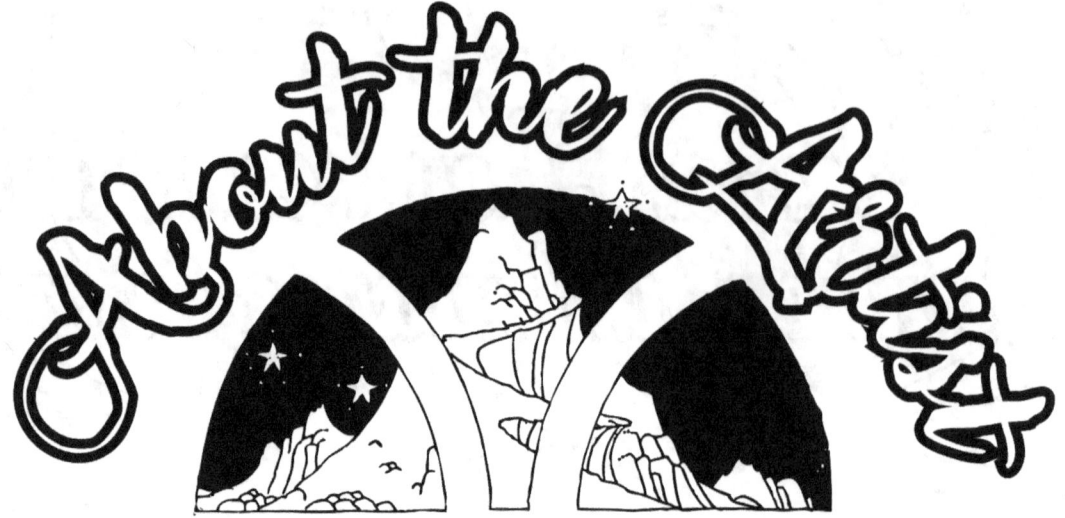

| Colored by | |
|---|---|
| On this day | |
| Notes | |
| | |
| | |
| | |

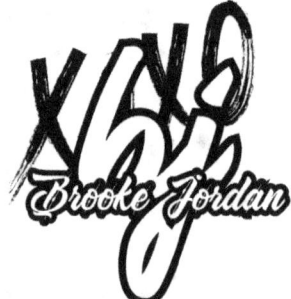

Amazon.com/author/bjos_Journals_etc

I suffer from
# SOBS
**STRESSED OUT BITCH**
syndrome

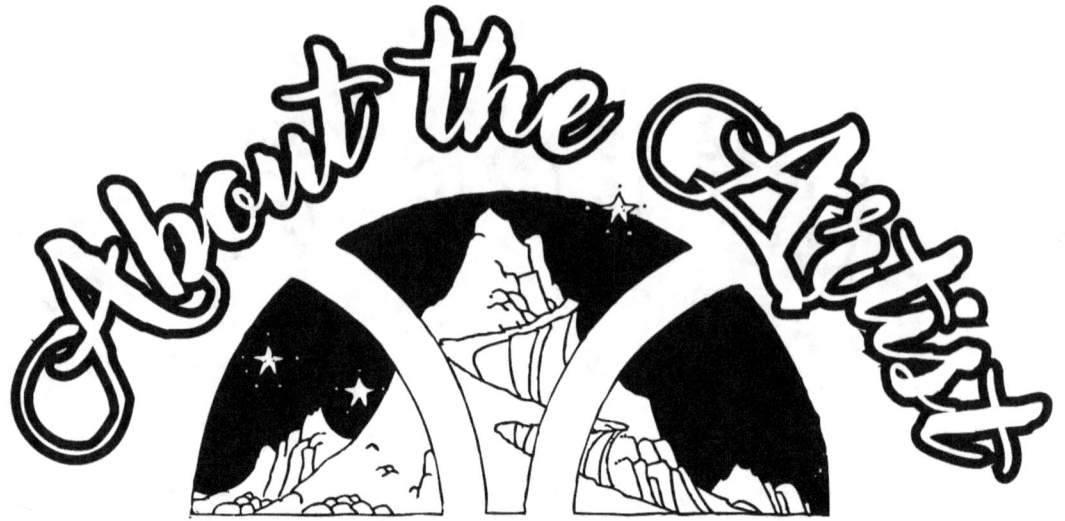

# About the Artist

| Colored by | |
| --- | --- |
| On this day | |
| Notes | |
| | |
| | |

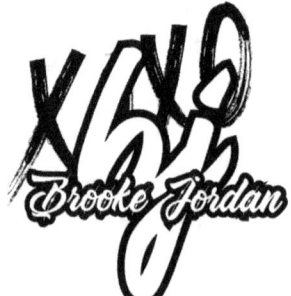

Brooke Jordan

Amazon.com/author/bjos_Journals_etc

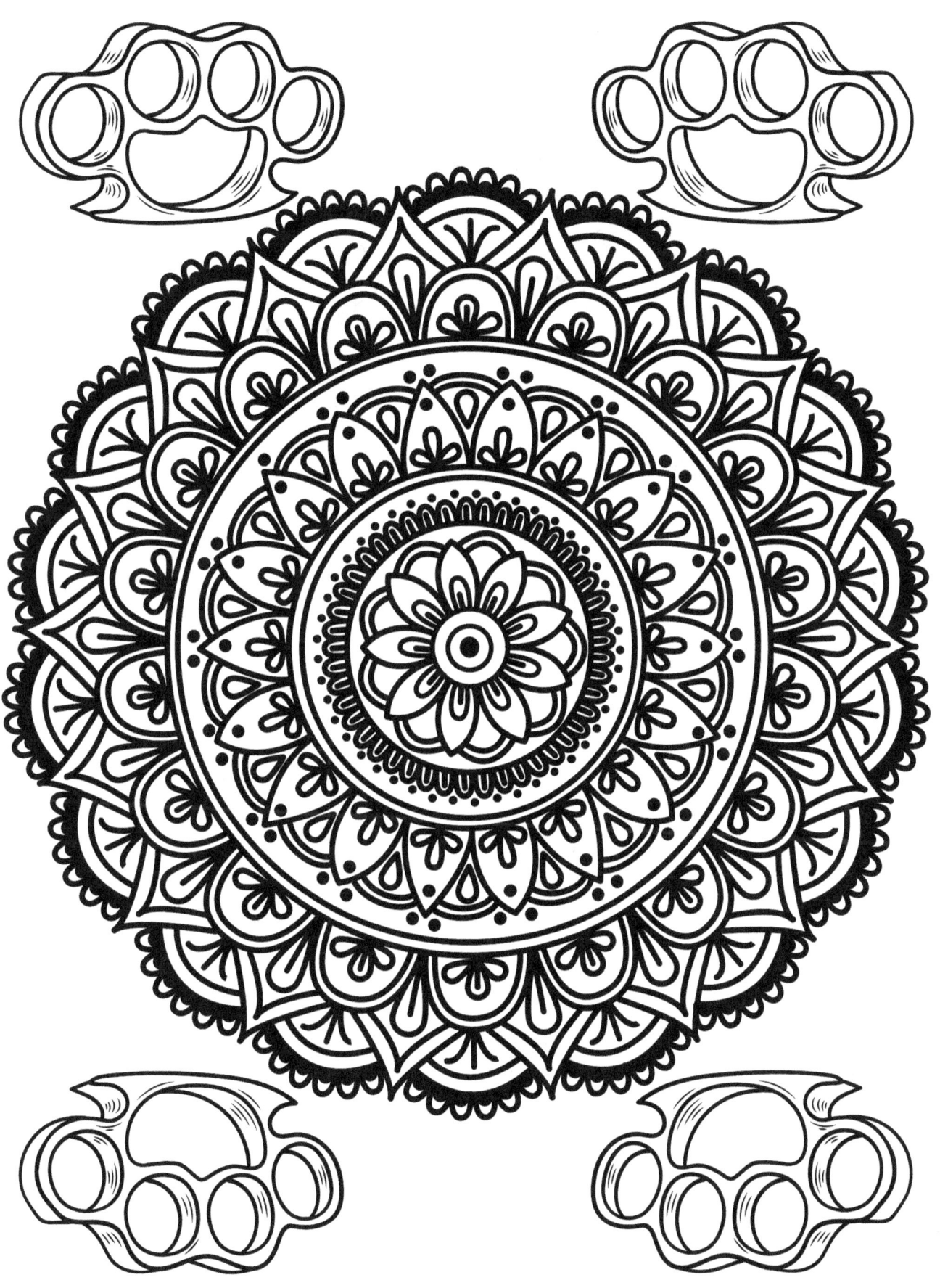

# About the Artist

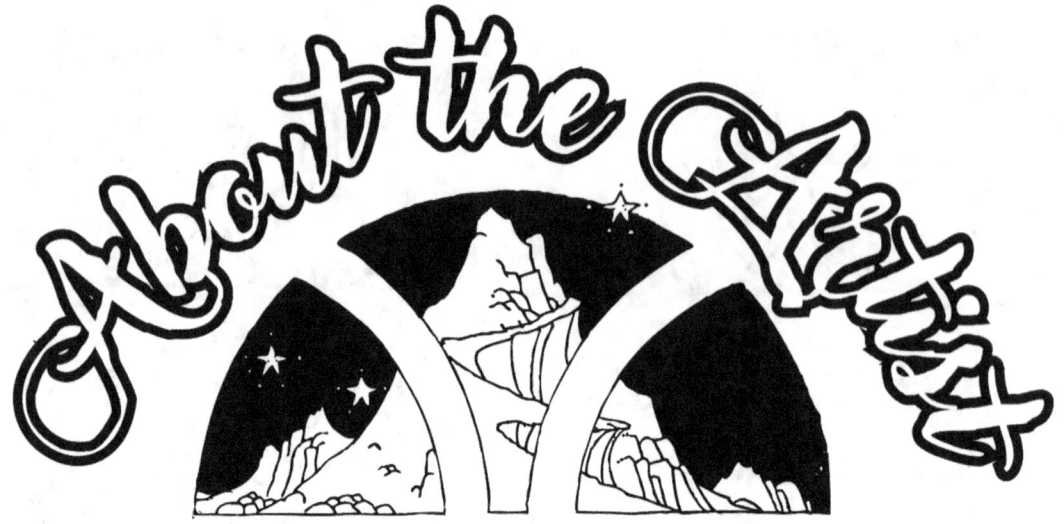

|  |  |
|---|---|
| Colored by |  |
| On this day |  |
| Notes |  |

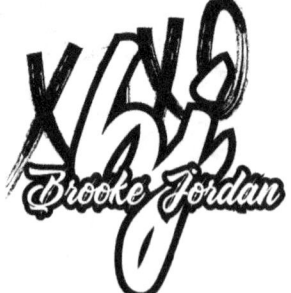

Amazon.com/author/bjos_Journals_etc

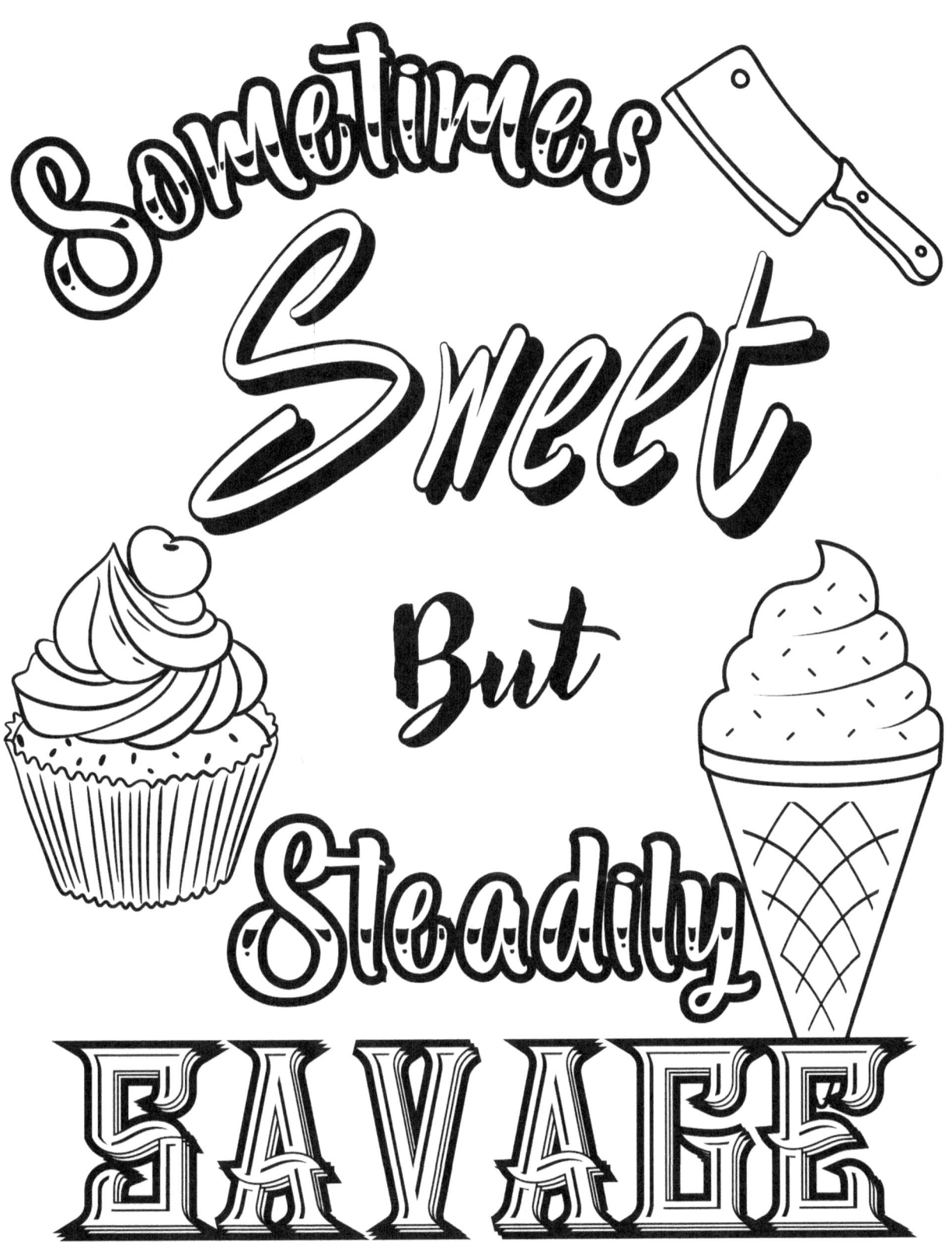

# About the Artist

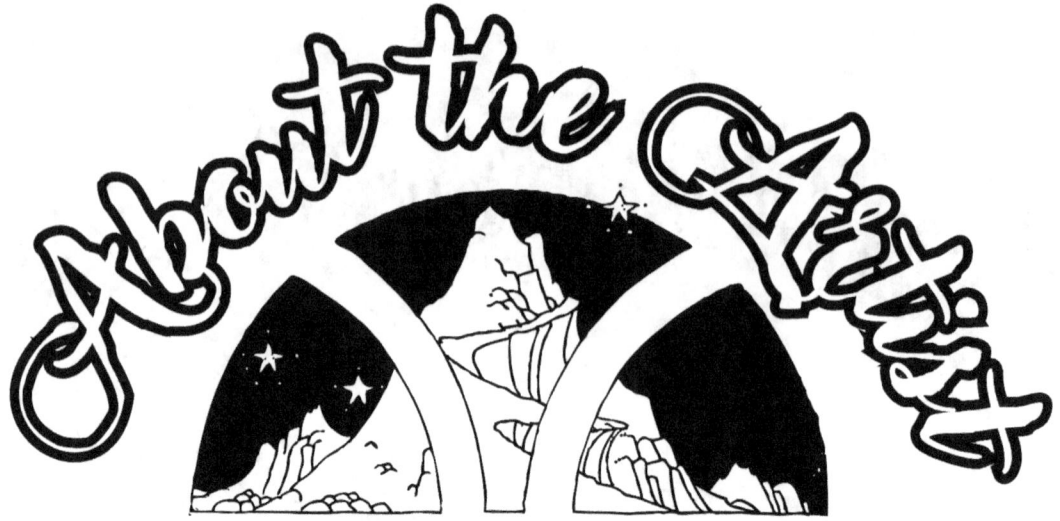

| | |
|---|---|
| Colored by | |
| On this day | |
| Notes | |

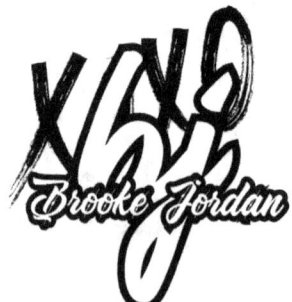

Brooke Jordan

Amazon.com/author/bjos_Journals_etc

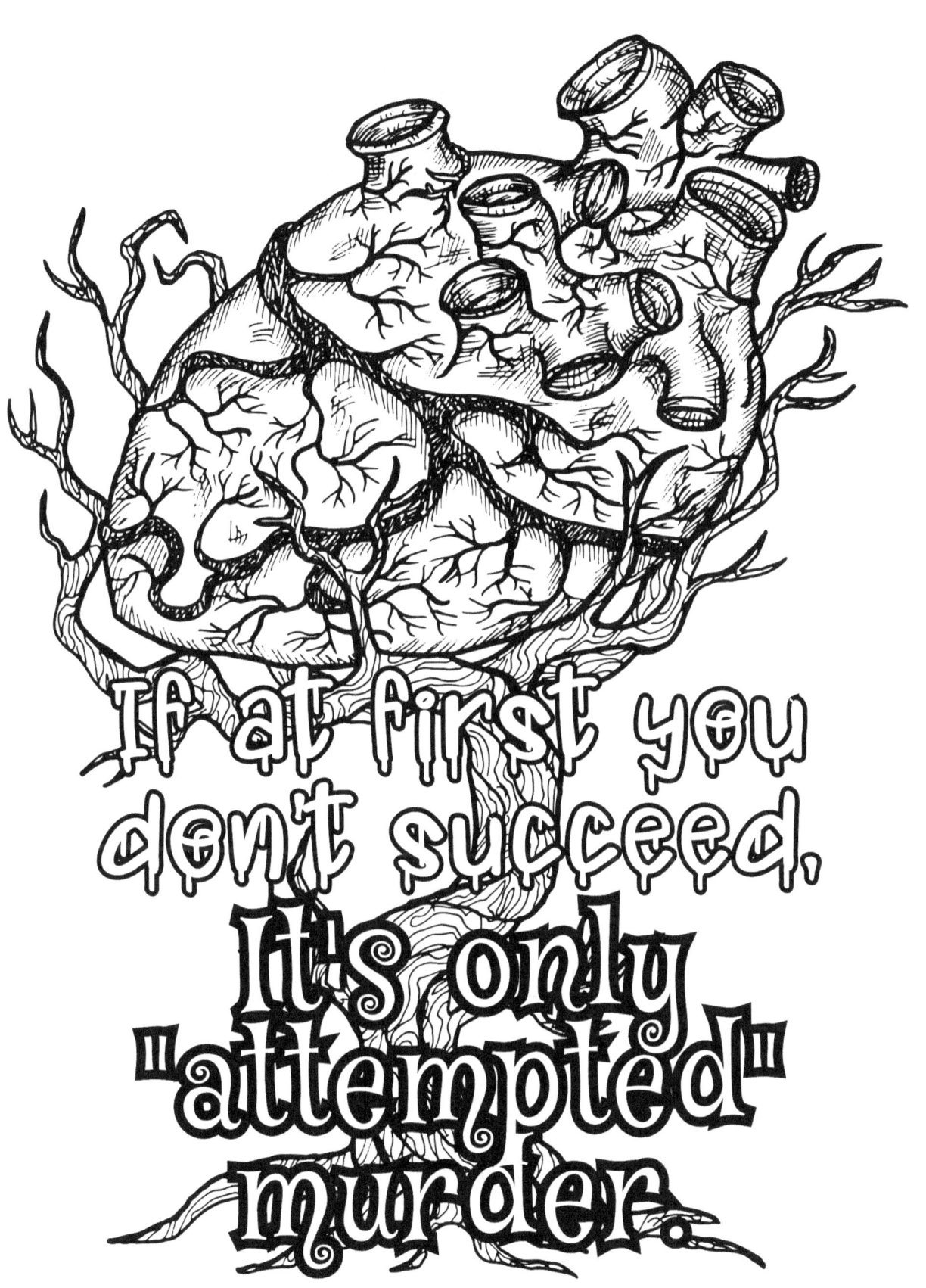

# About the Artist

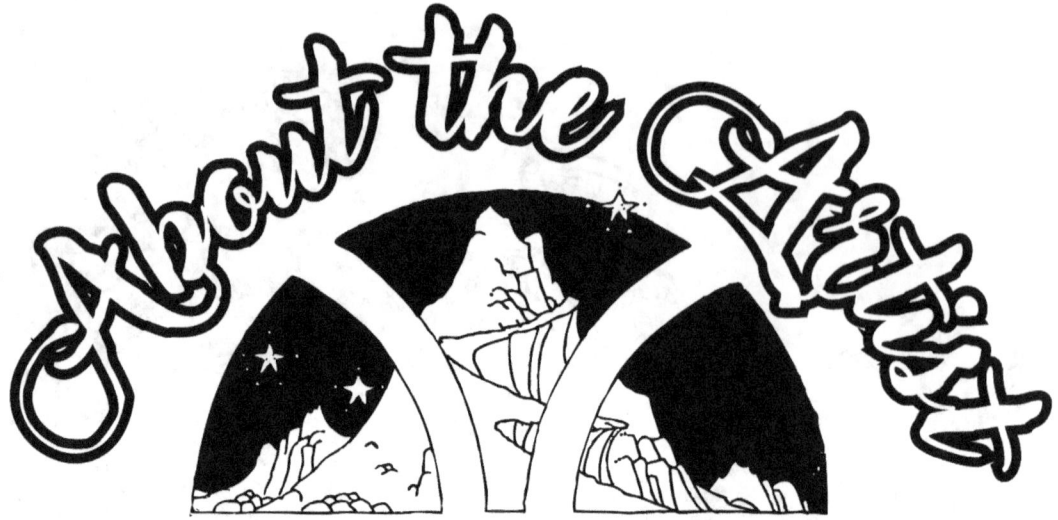

| | |
|---|---|
| Colored by | |
| On this day | |
| Notes | |

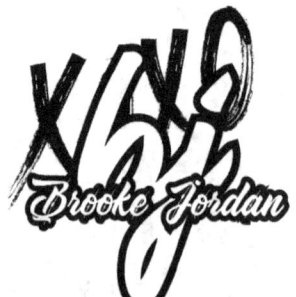

Brooke Jordan

Amazon.com/author/bjos_Journals_etc

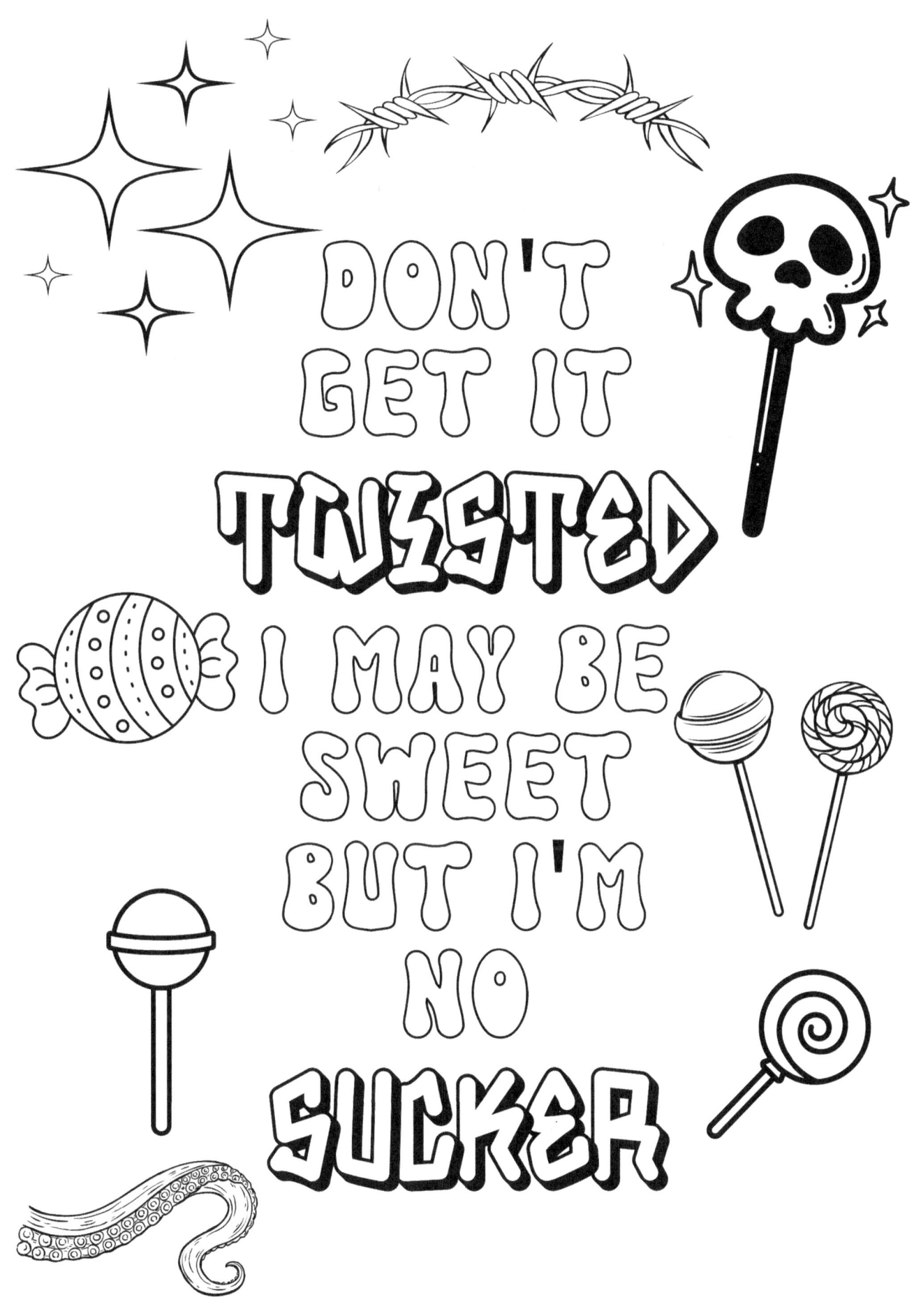

# About the Artist

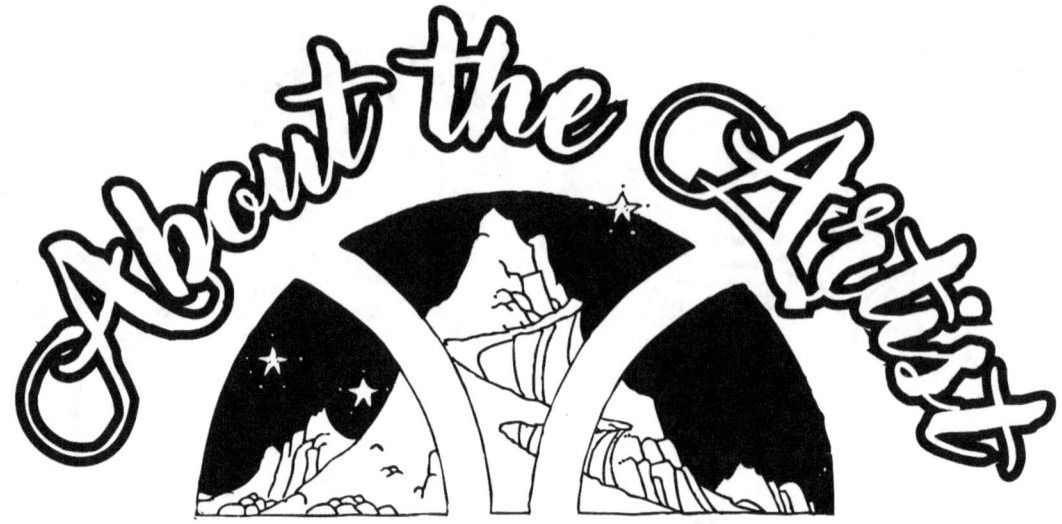

| Colored by | |
|---|---|
| On this day | |
| Notes | |

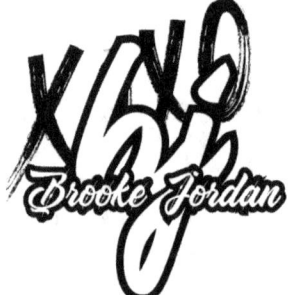

Amazon.com/author/bjos_Journals_etc

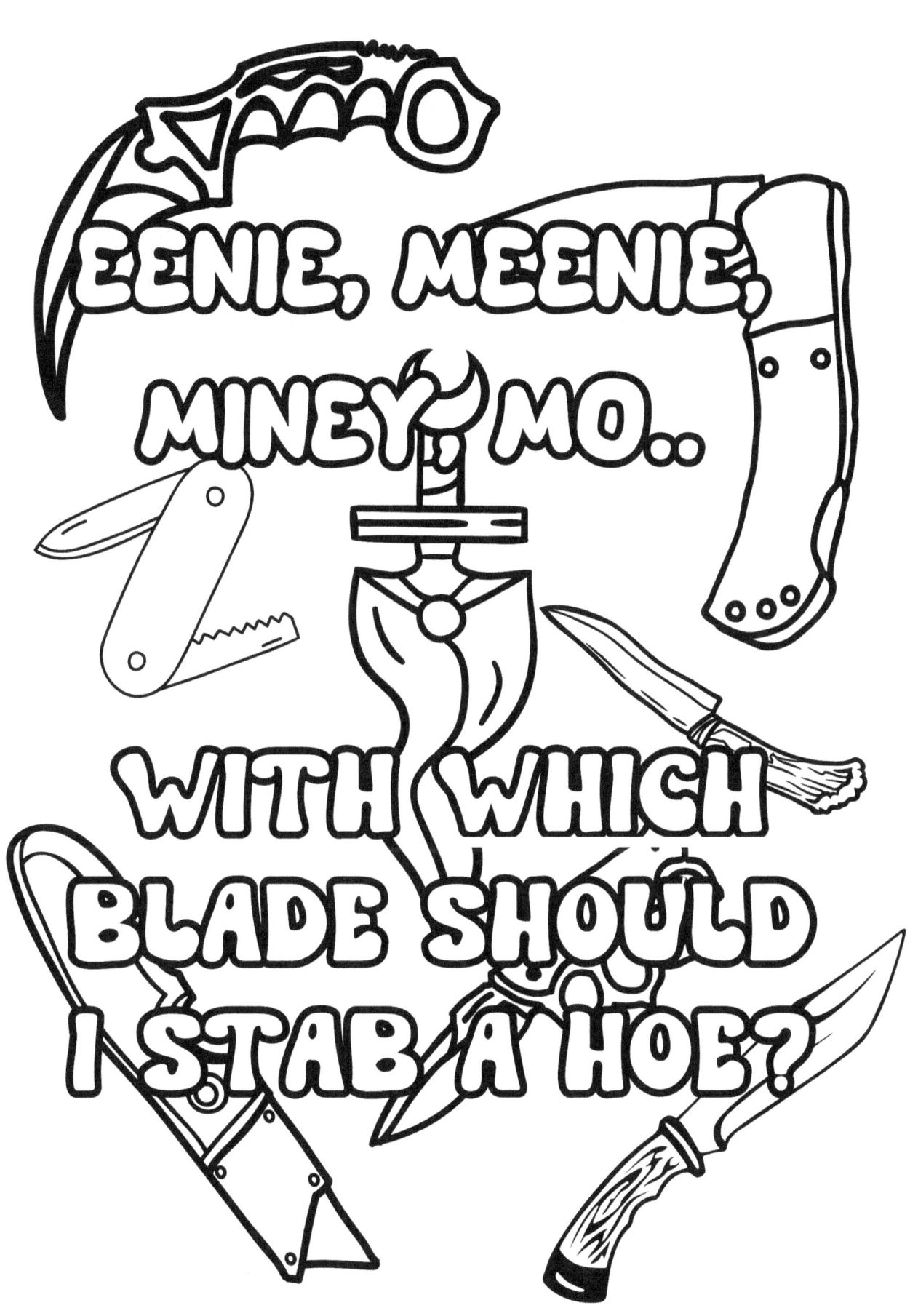

# About the Artist

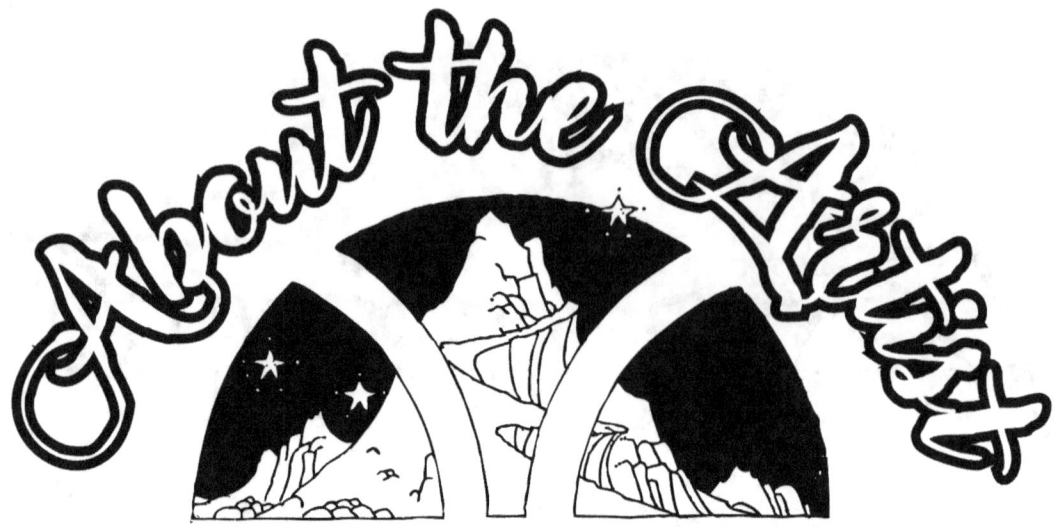

| | |
|---|---|
| Colored by | |
| On this day | |
| Notes | |

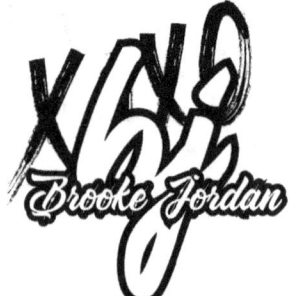

Brooke Jordan

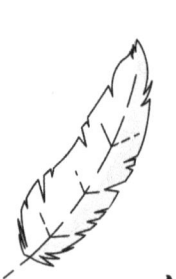

Amazon.com/author/bjos_Journals_etc

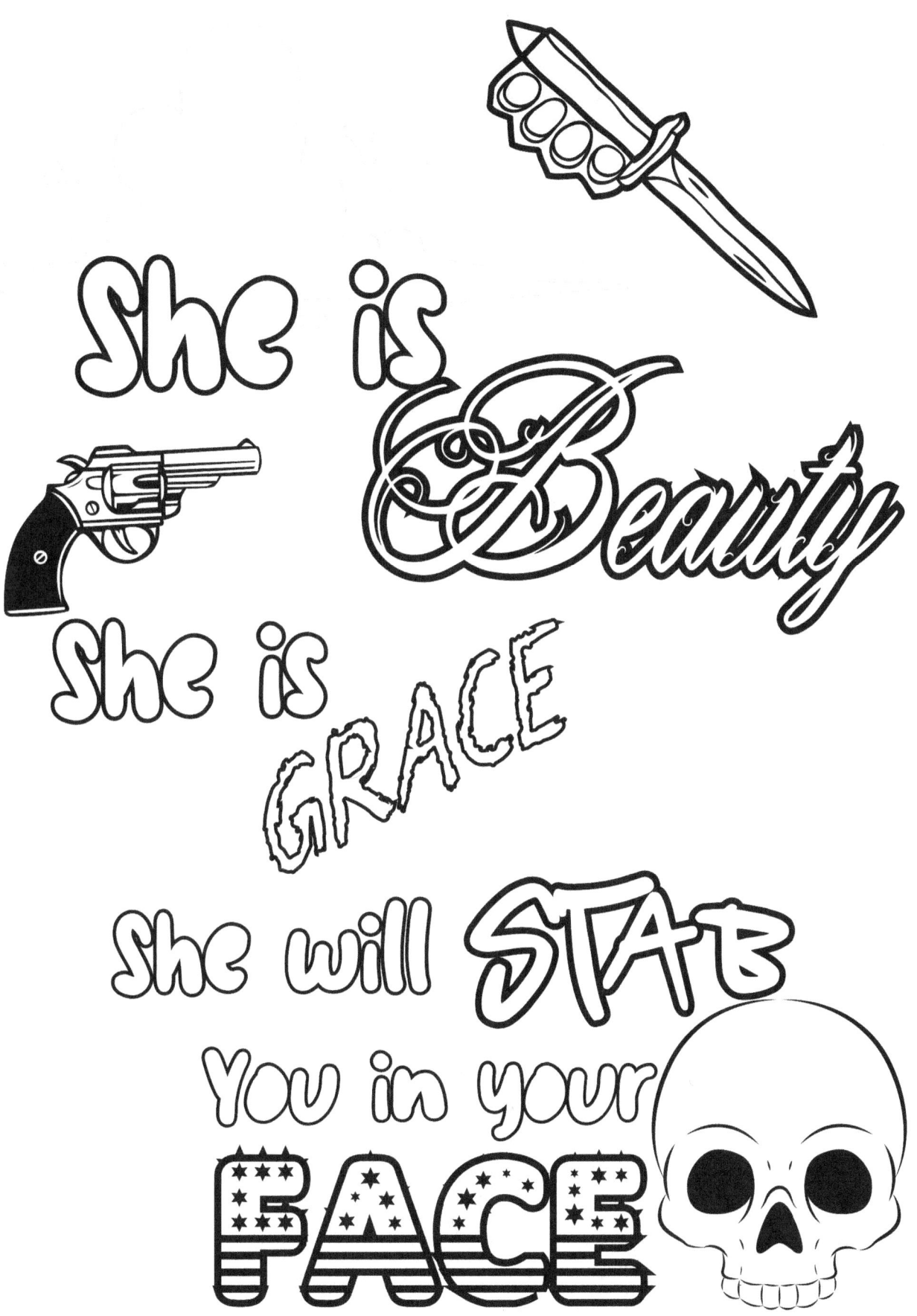

# About the Artist

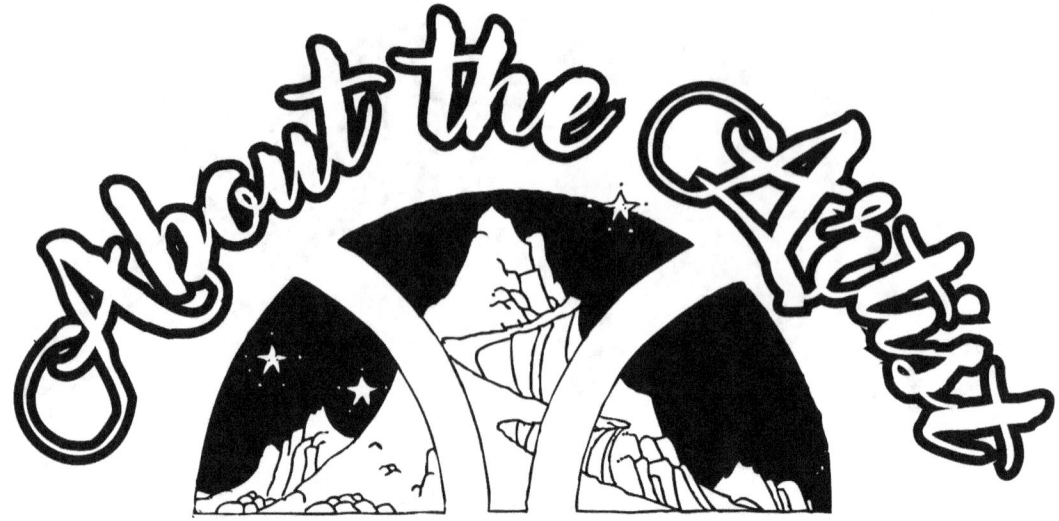

| Colored by | |
|---|---|
| On this day | |
| Notes | |

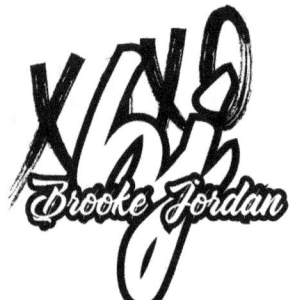

Amazon.com/author/bjos_Journals_etc

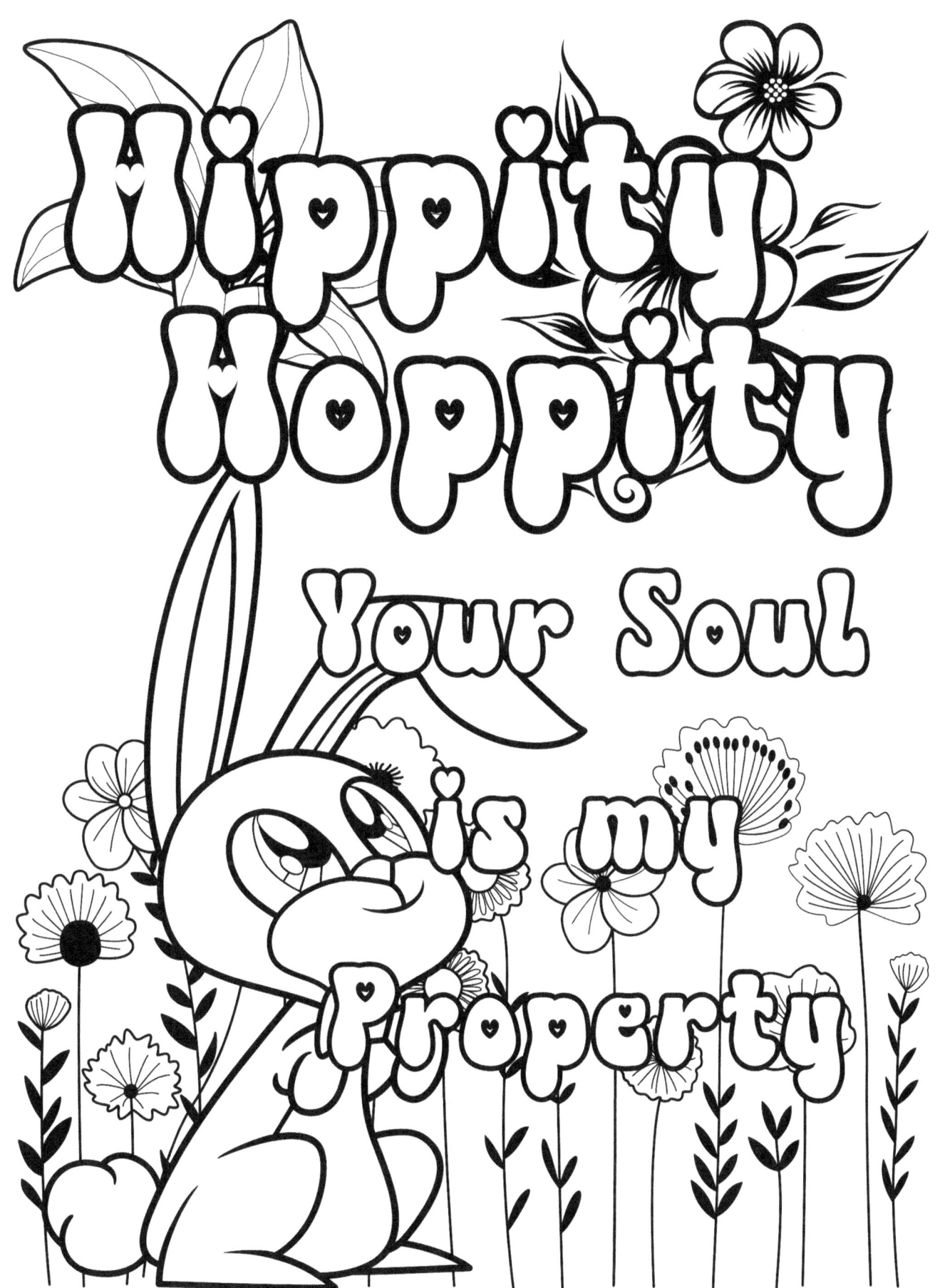

# About the Artist

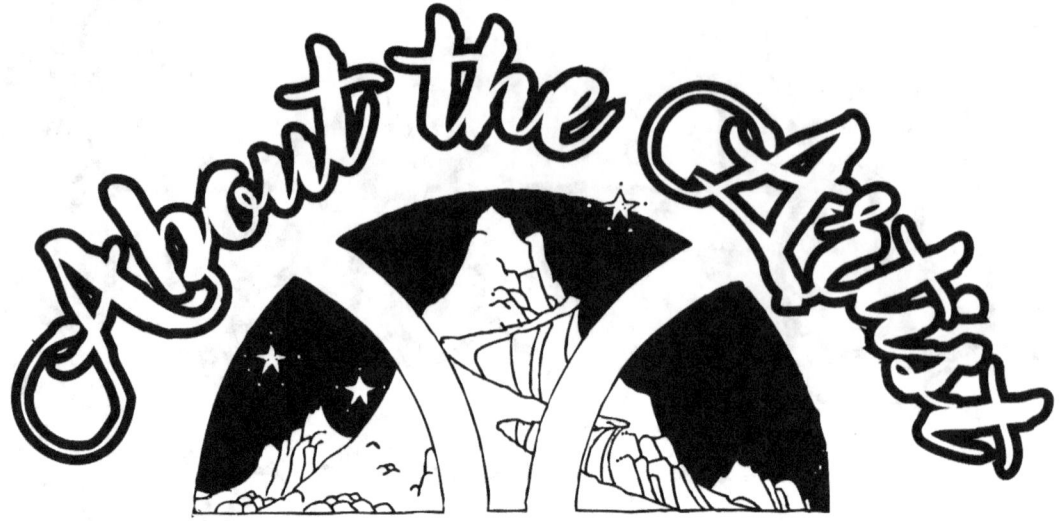

| | |
|---|---|
| Colored by | |
| On this day | |
| Notes | |

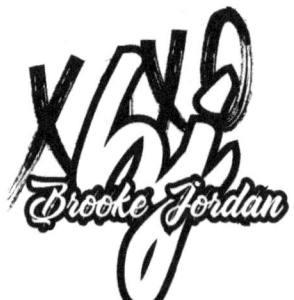

Amazon.com/author/bjos_Journals_etc

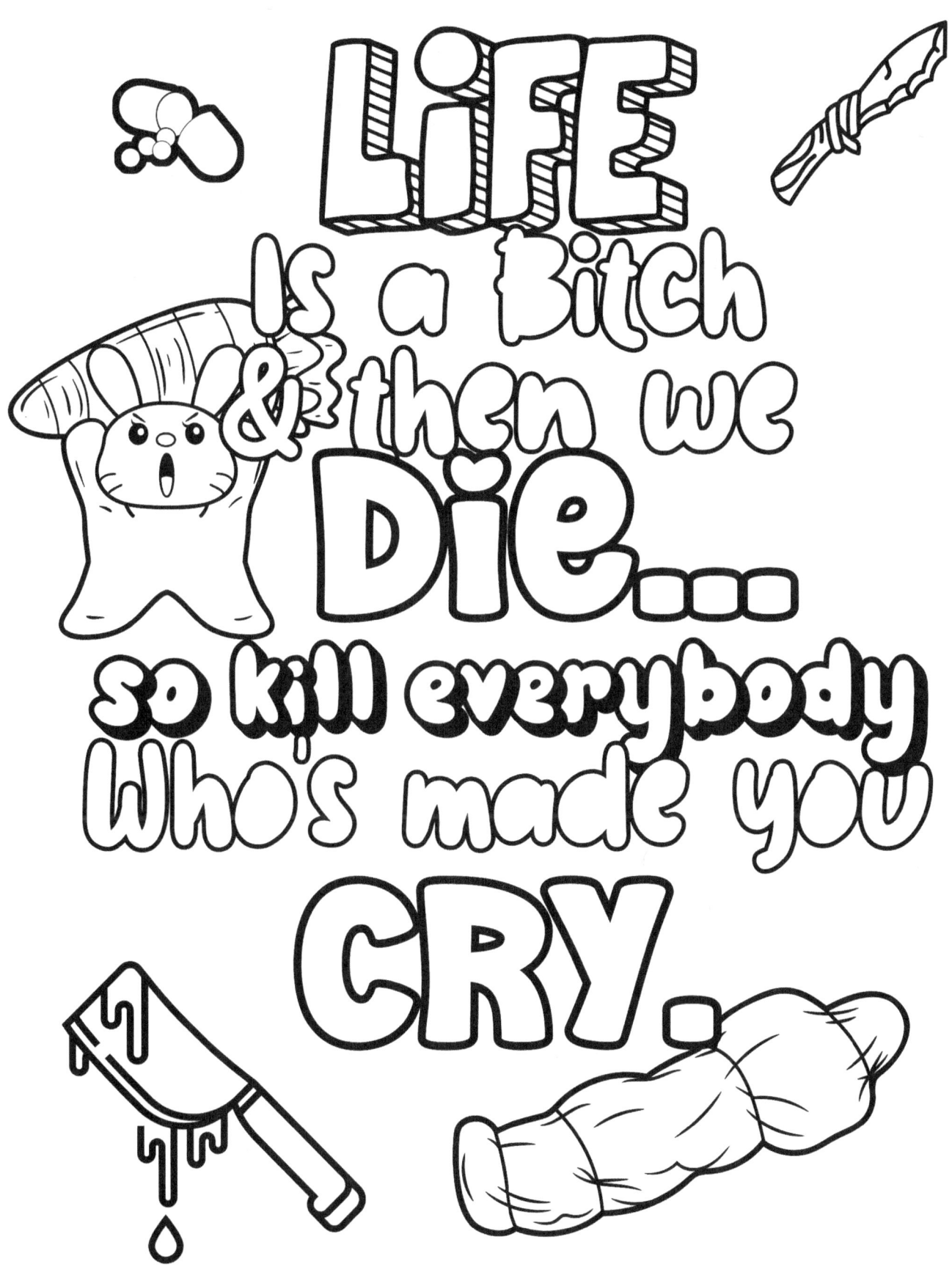

# About the Artist

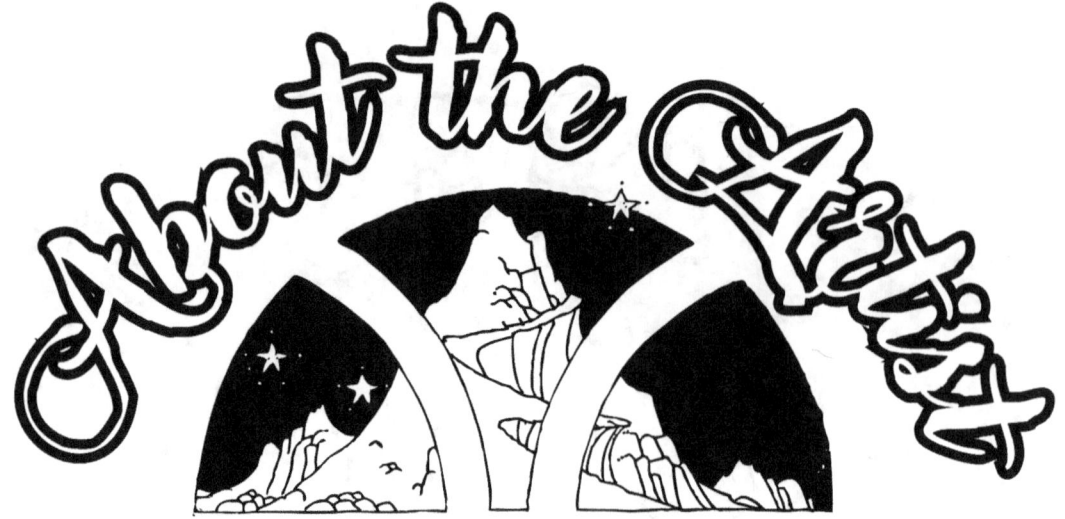

| Colored by | |
|---|---|
| On this day | |
| Notes | |

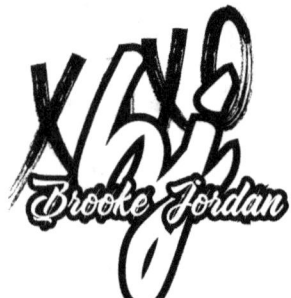

Amazon.com/author/bjos_Journals_etc

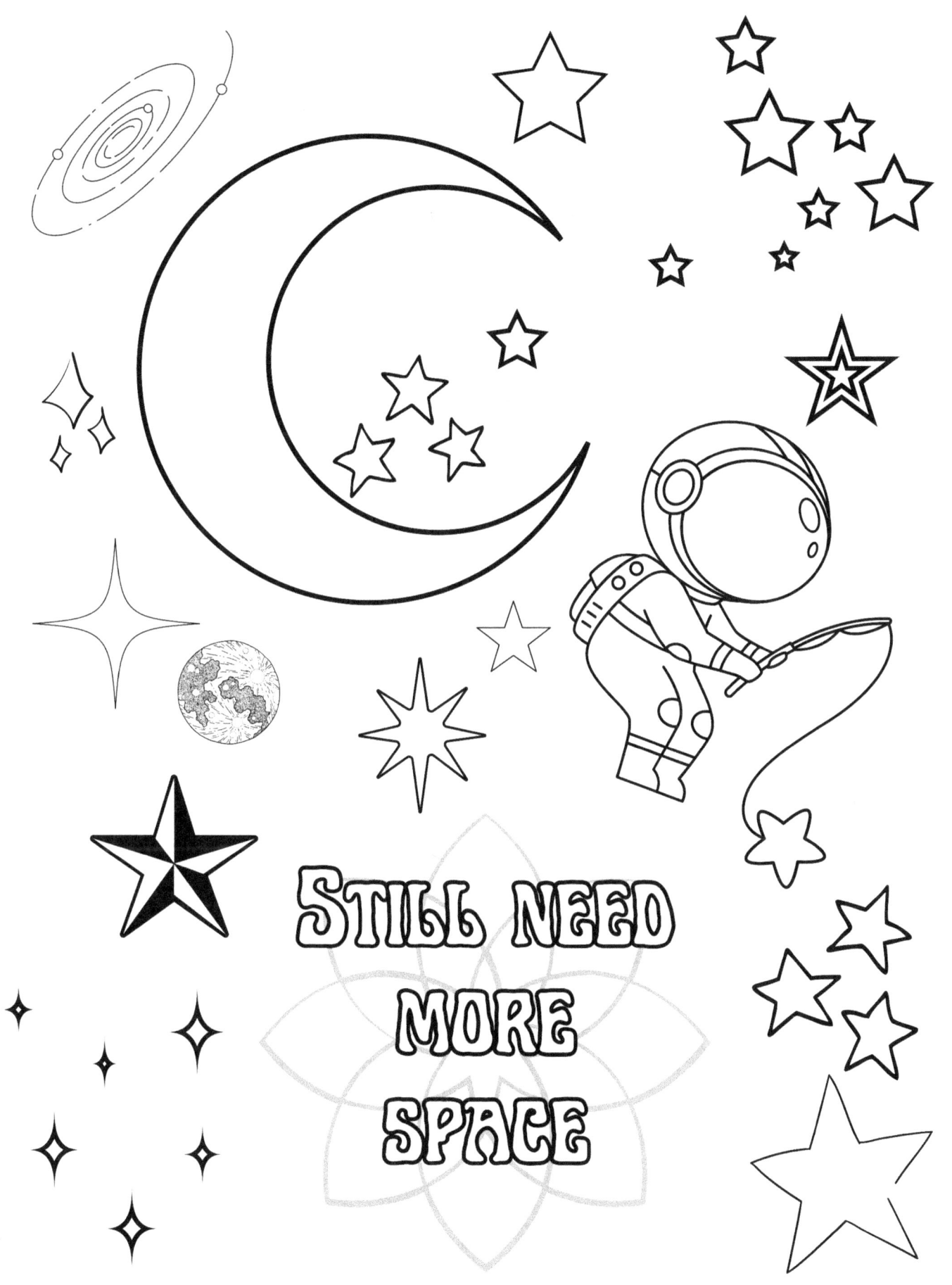

# About the Artist

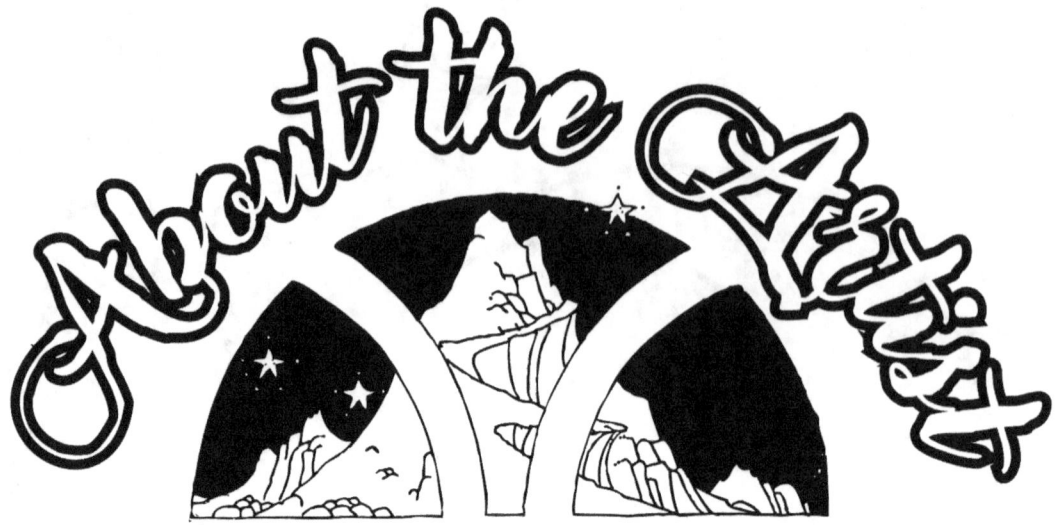

| Colored by | |
|---|---|
| On this day | |
| Notes | |

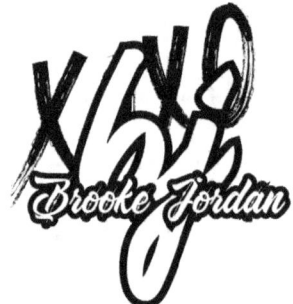

Amazon.com/author/bjos_Journals_etc

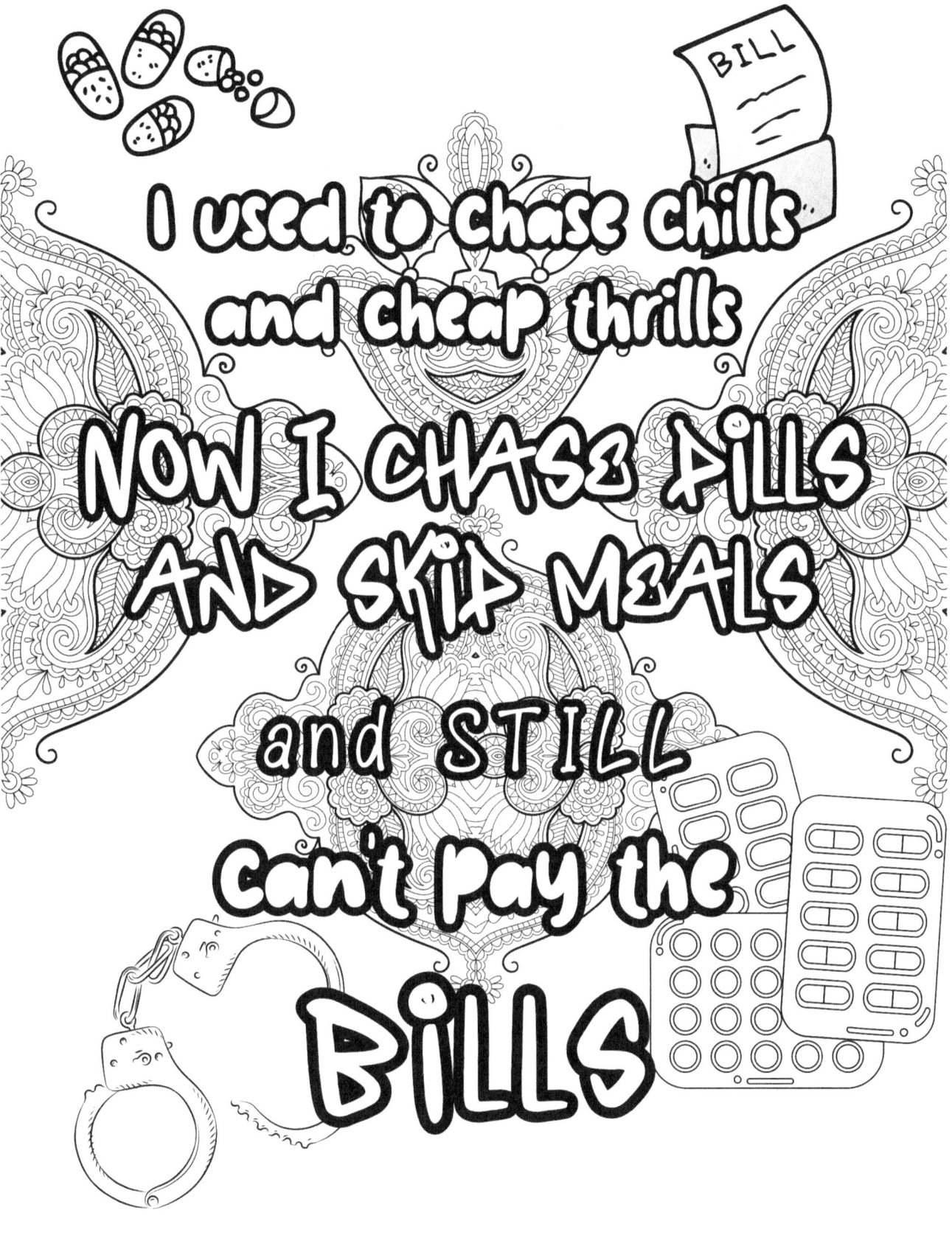

# About the Artist

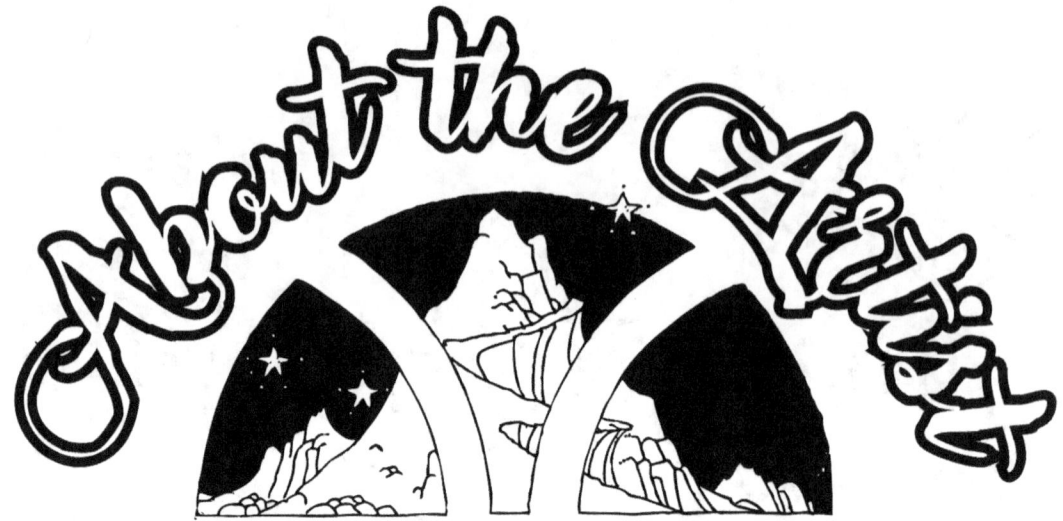

| Colored by | |
|---|---|
| On this day | |
| Notes | |

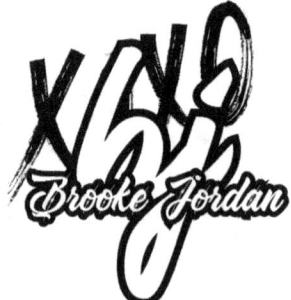

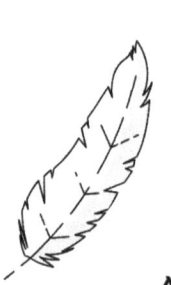

Amazon.com/author/bjos_Journals_etc

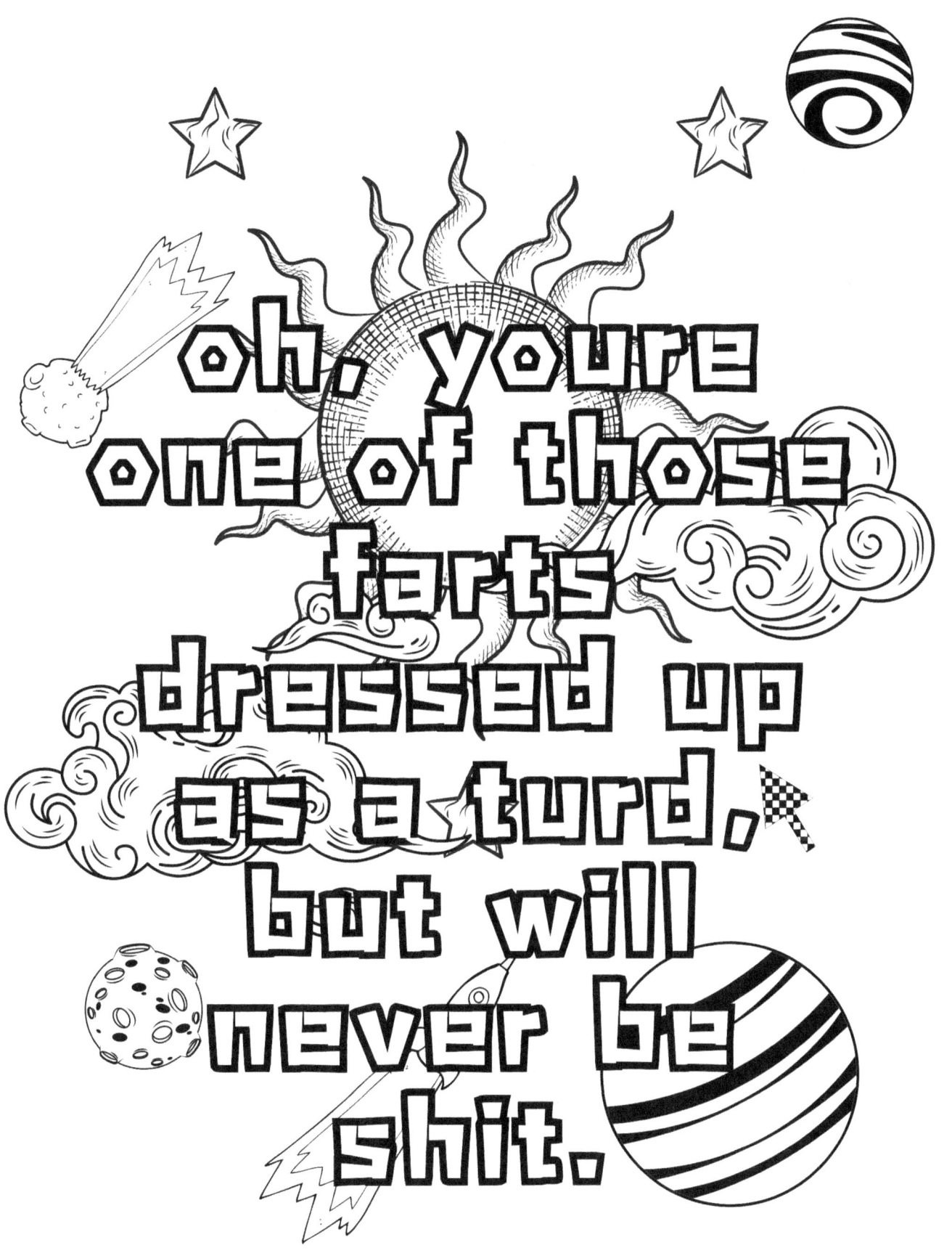

# About the Artist

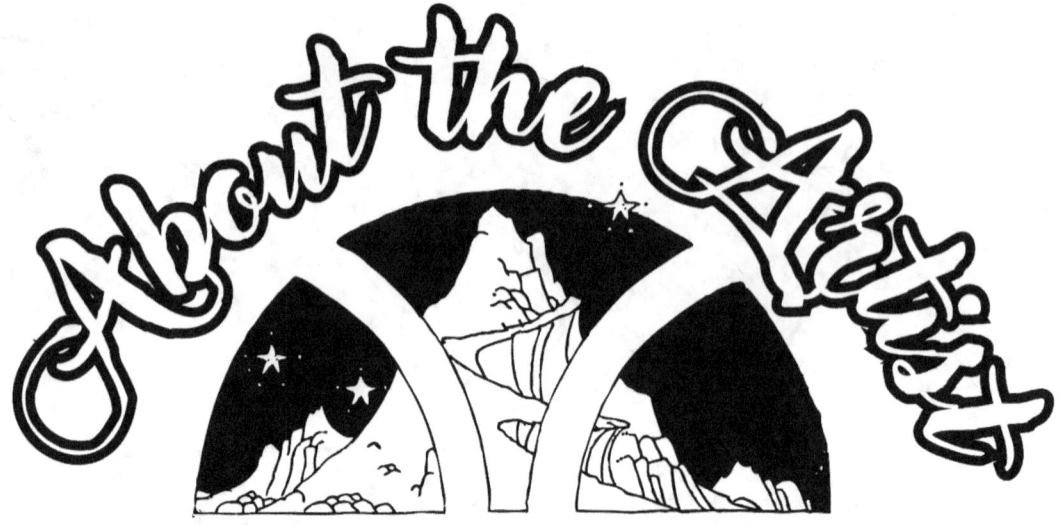

| Colored by | |
|---|---|
| On this day | |
| Notes | |

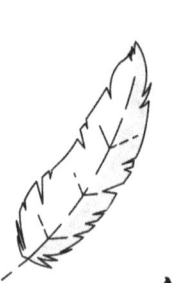
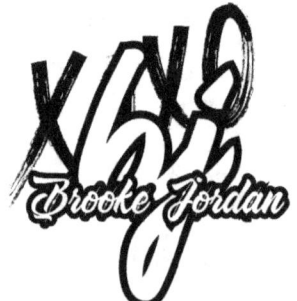

Amazon.com/author/bjos_Journals_etc

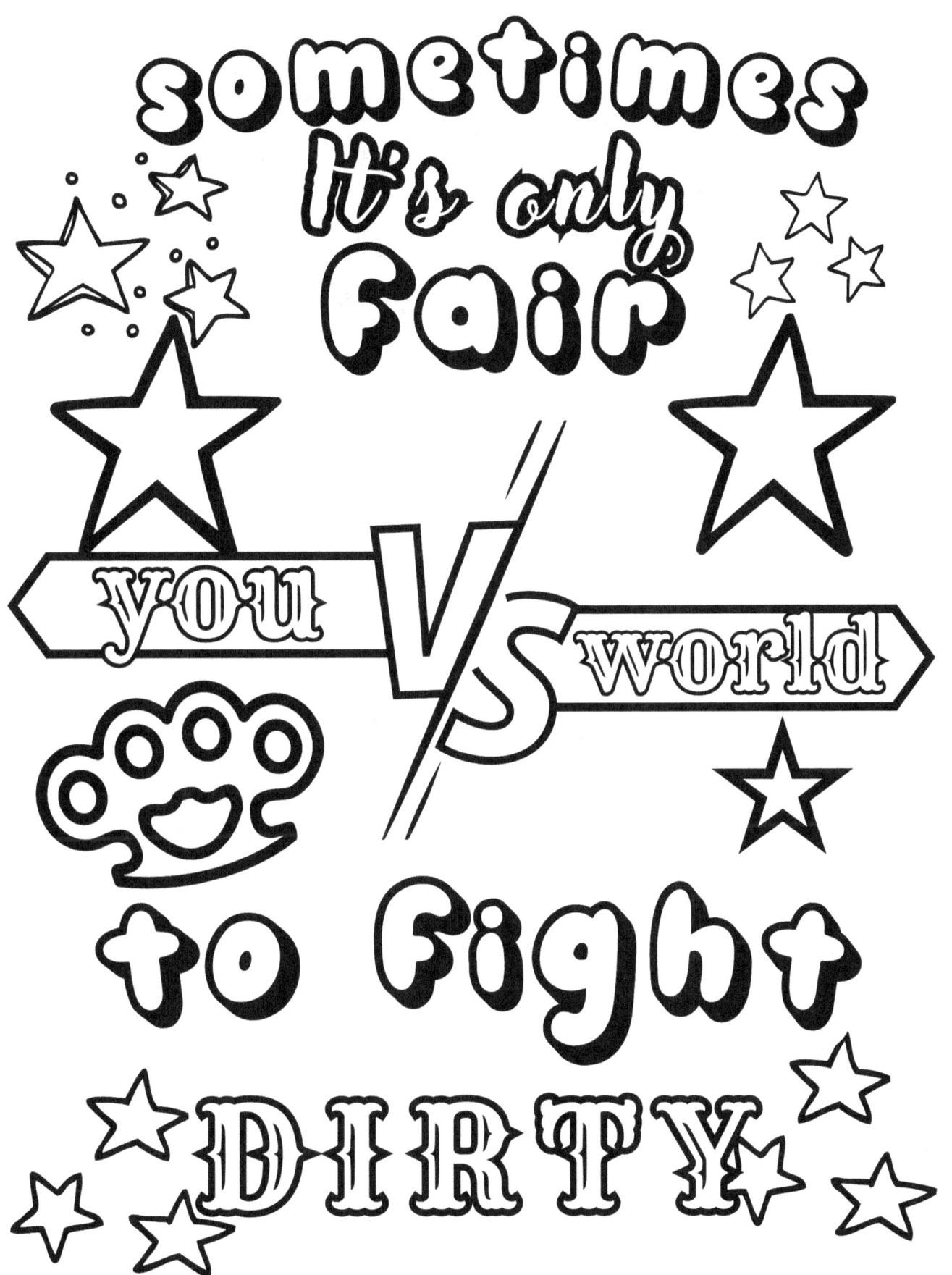

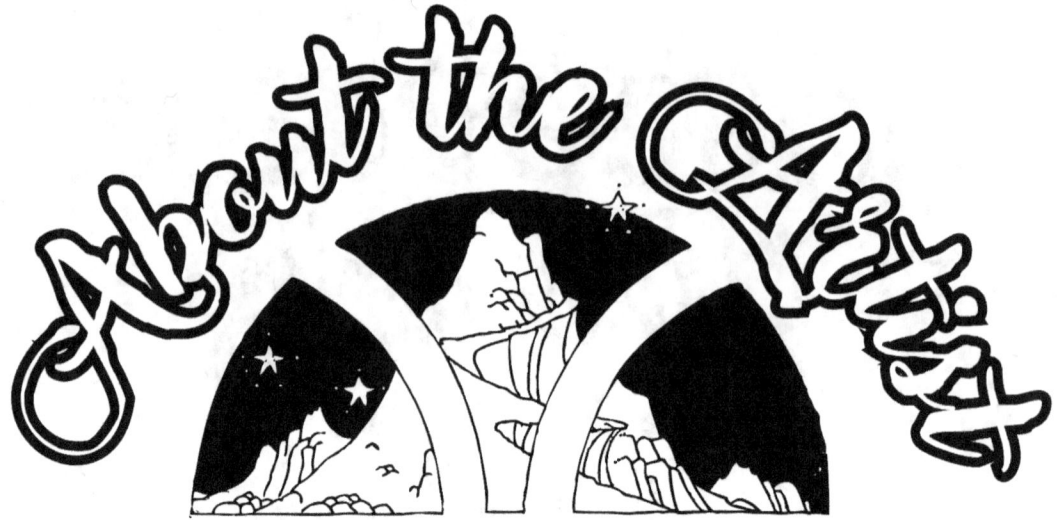

# About the Artist

| Colored by | |
| --- | --- |
| On this day | |
| Notes | |

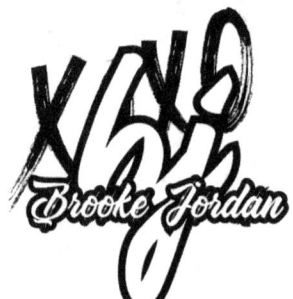

Amazon.com/author/bjos_Journals_etc

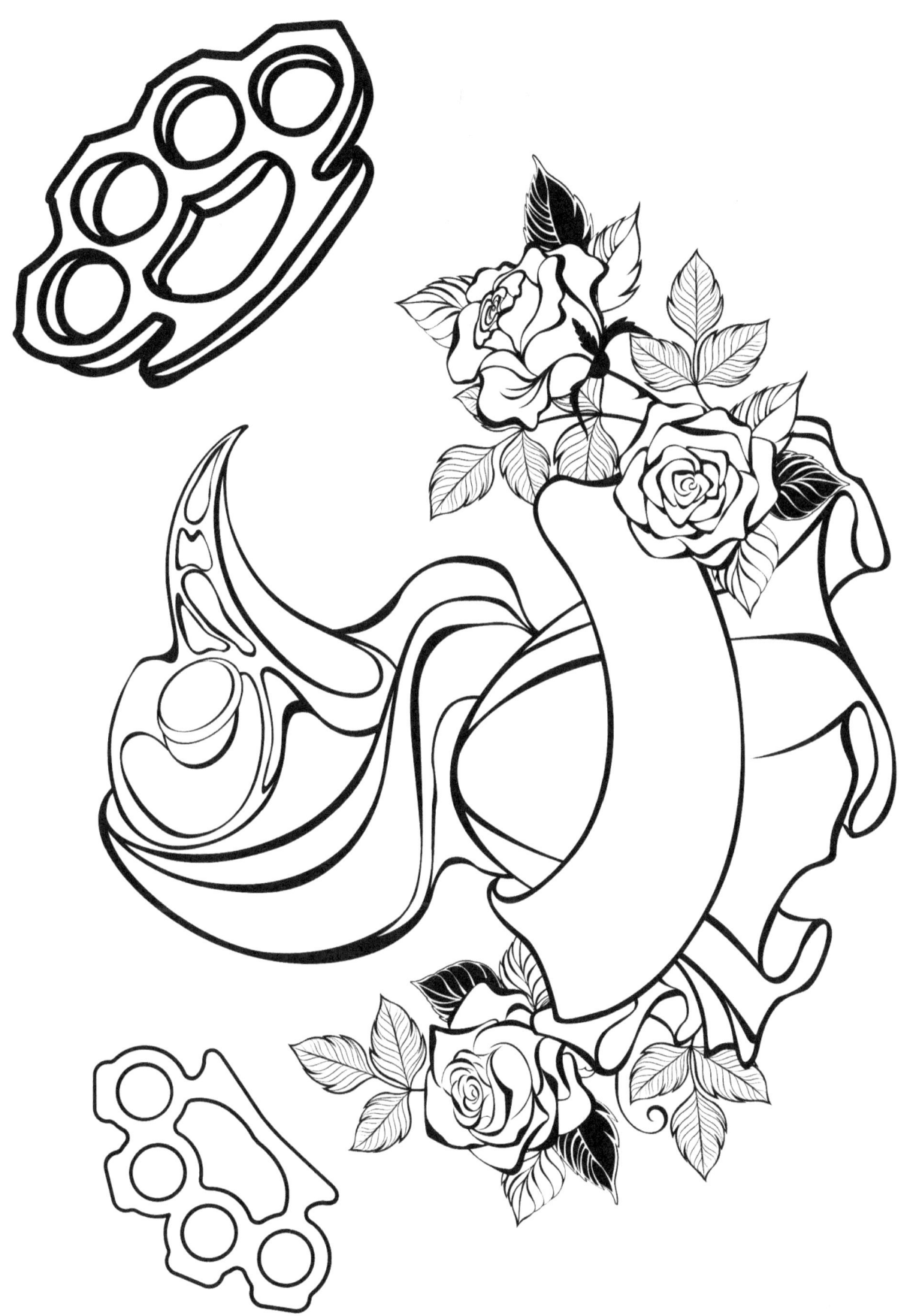

# About the Artist

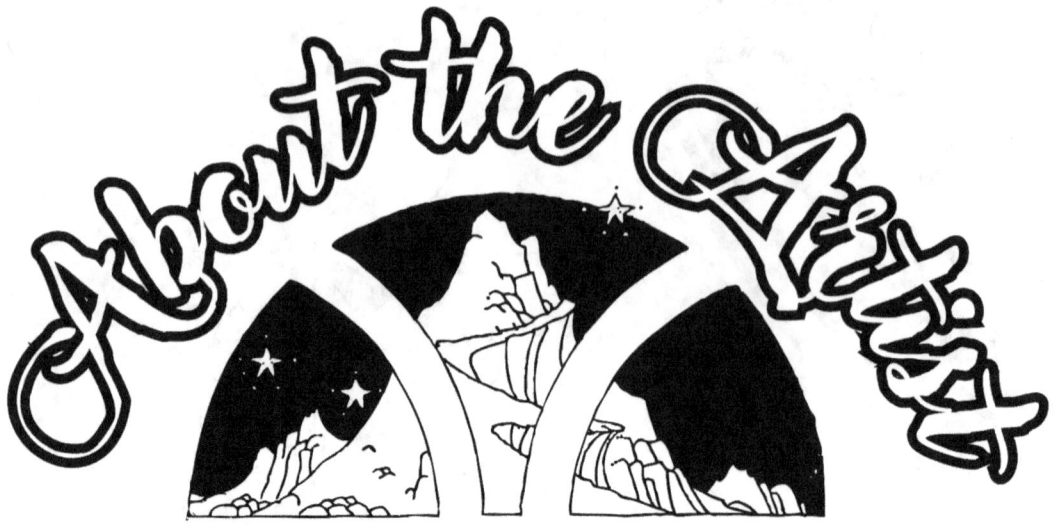

| | |
|---|---|
| Colored by | |
| On this day | |
| Notes | |

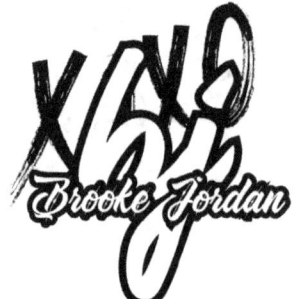

Amazon.com/author/bjos_Journals_etc

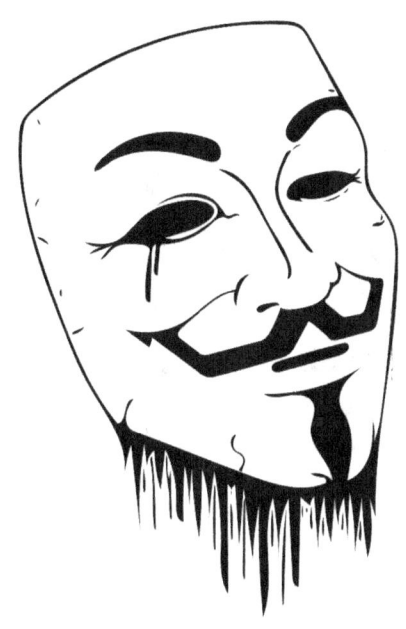

My love is like a candle

If you FORGET about ME I'll burn your HOUSE DOWN

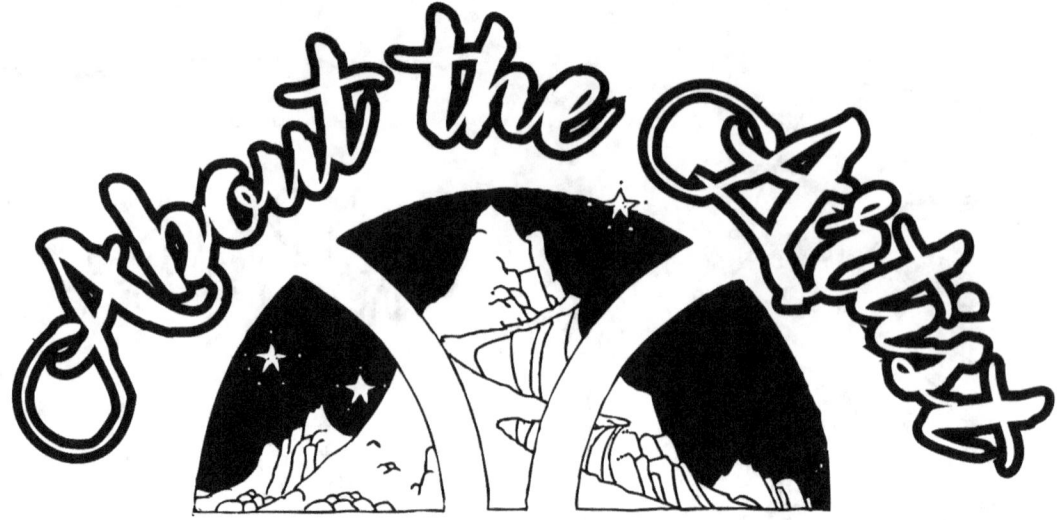

# About the Artist

| Colored by | |
| --- | --- |
| On this day | |
| Notes | |

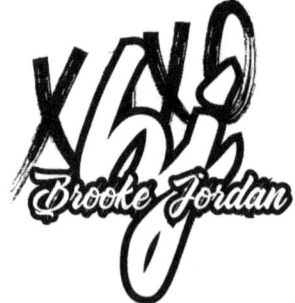

Amazon.com/author/bjos_Journals_etc

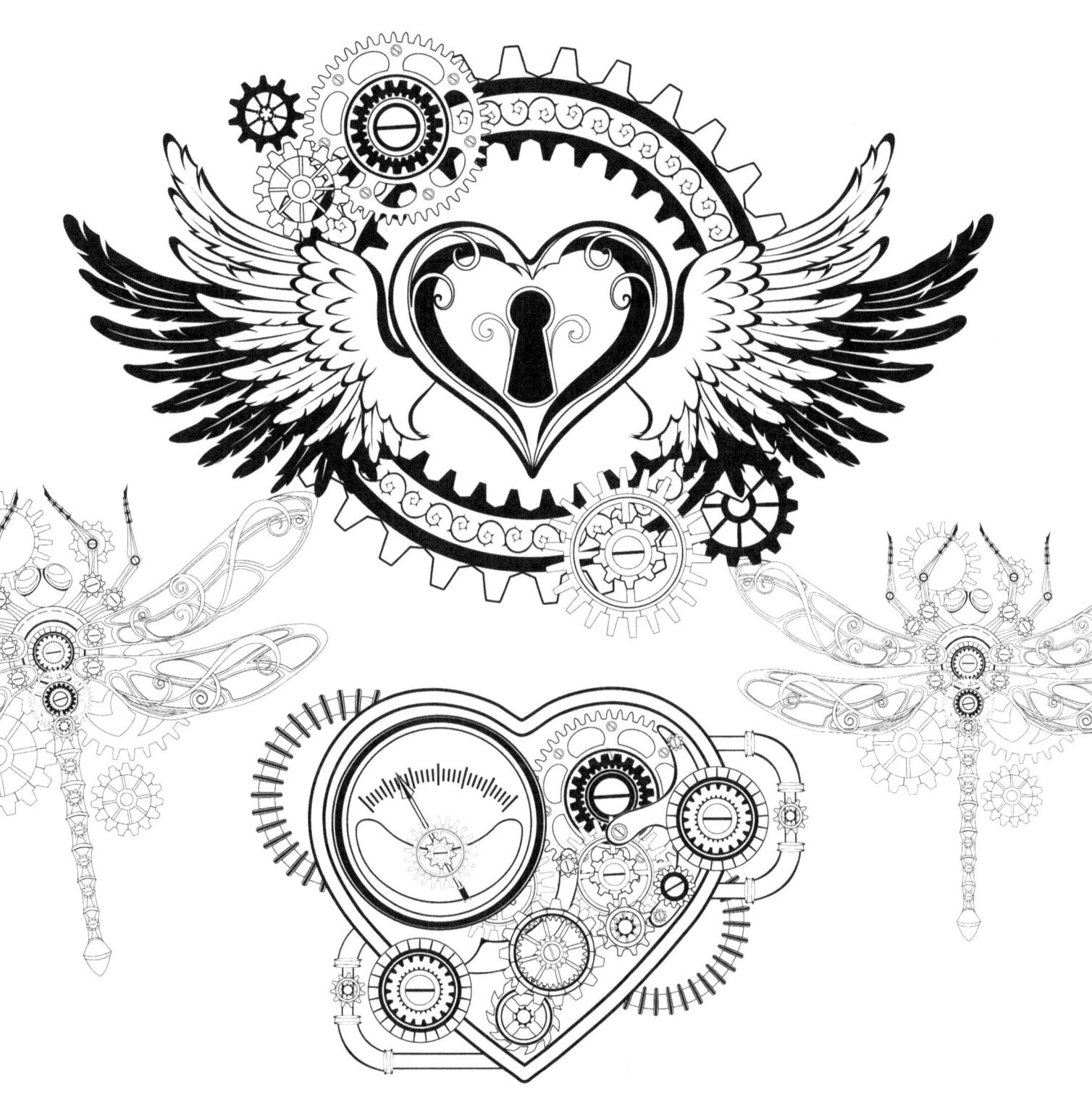

# About the Artist

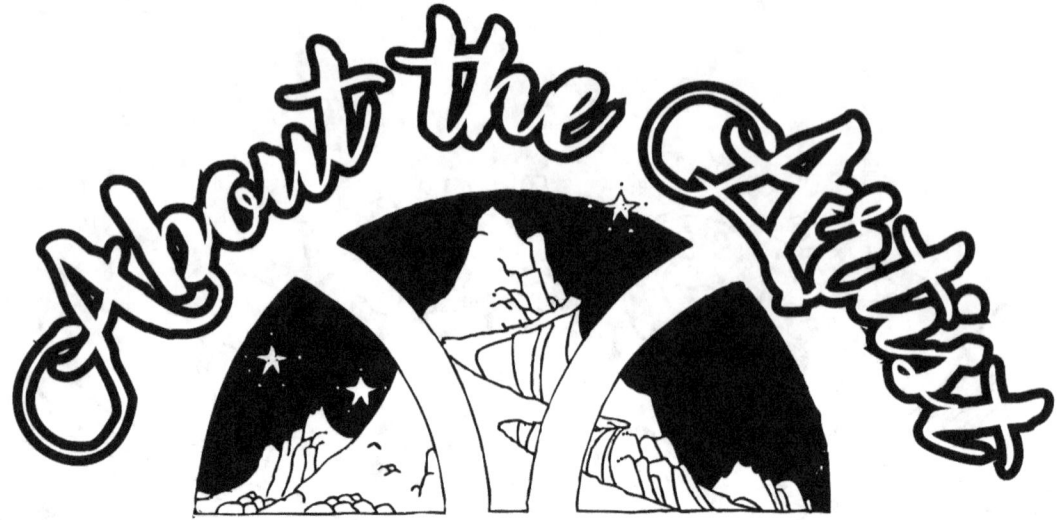

| | |
|---|---|
| Colored by | |
| On this day | |
| Notes | |

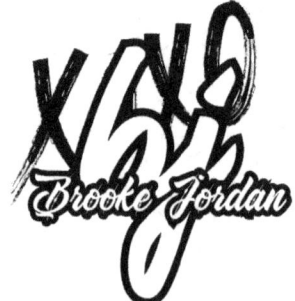

Brooke Jordan

Amazon.com/author/bjos_Journals_etc

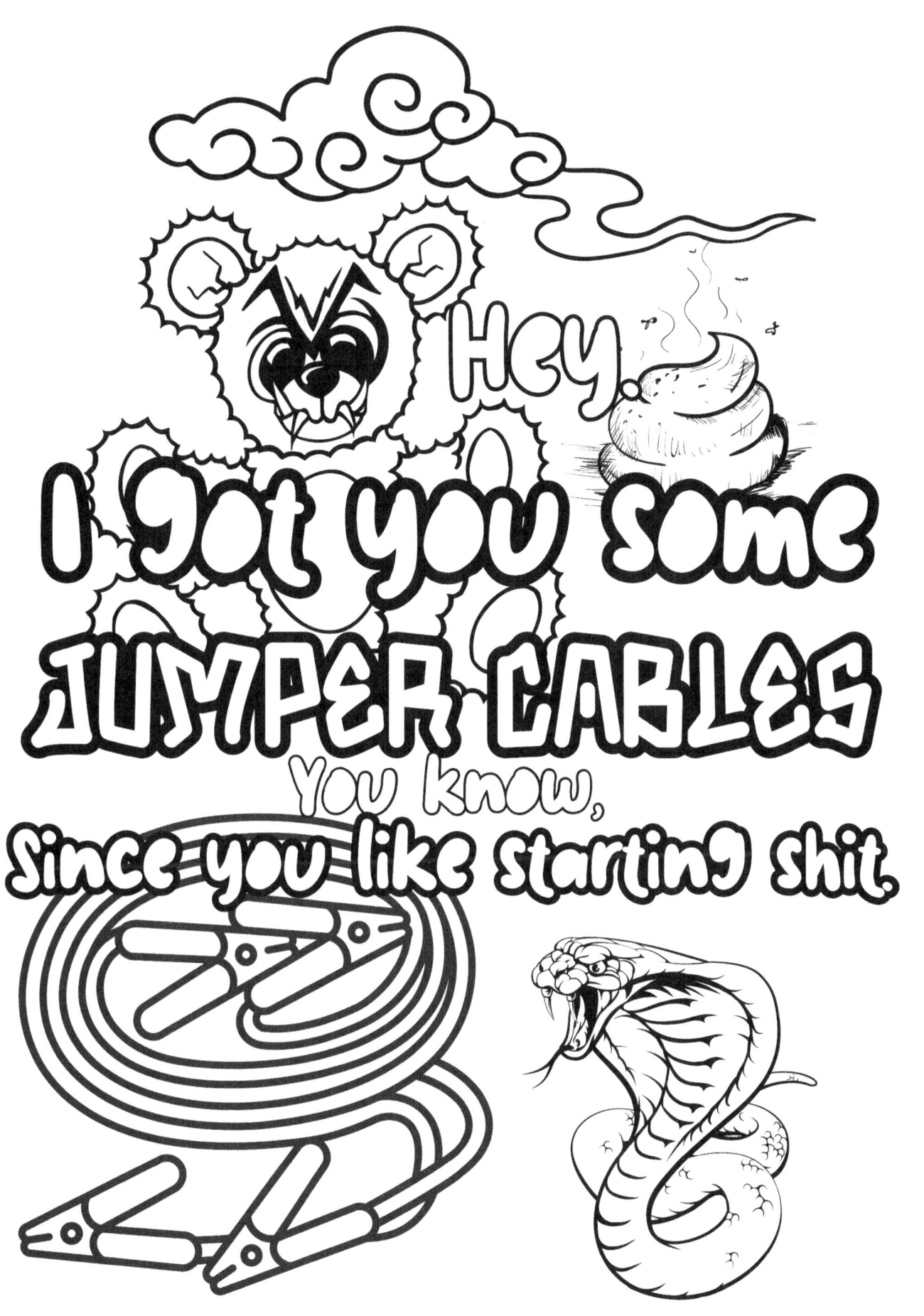

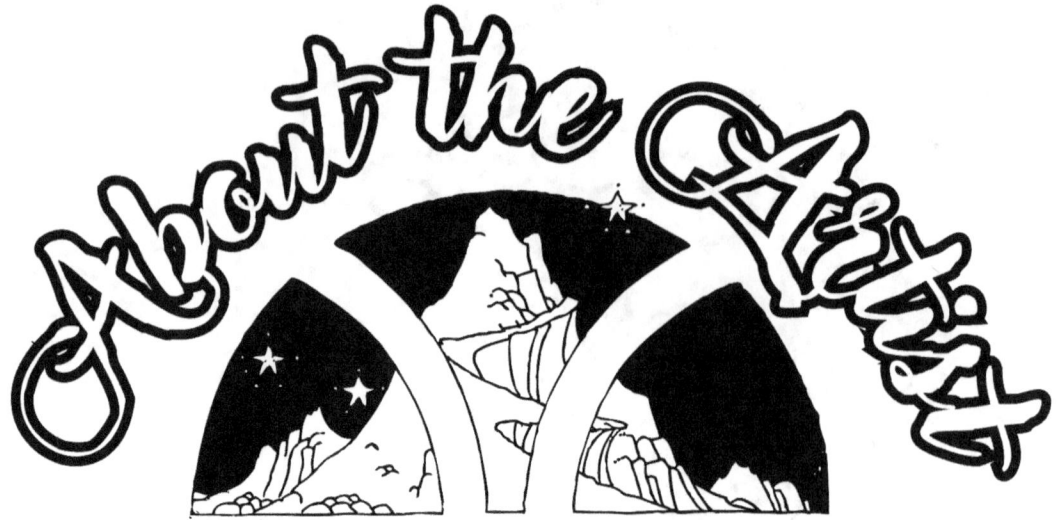

# About the Artist

| Colored by | |
| --- | --- |
| On this day | |
| Notes | |
| | |
| | |
| | |

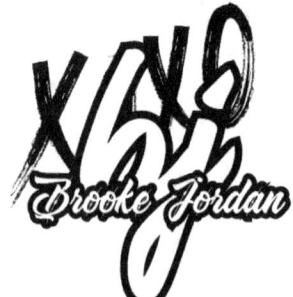

Brooke Jordan

Amazon.com/author/bjos_Journals_etc

HERE LIE MY INTEGRITY, GOOD INTENTIONS, & SHITS I ONCE GAVE

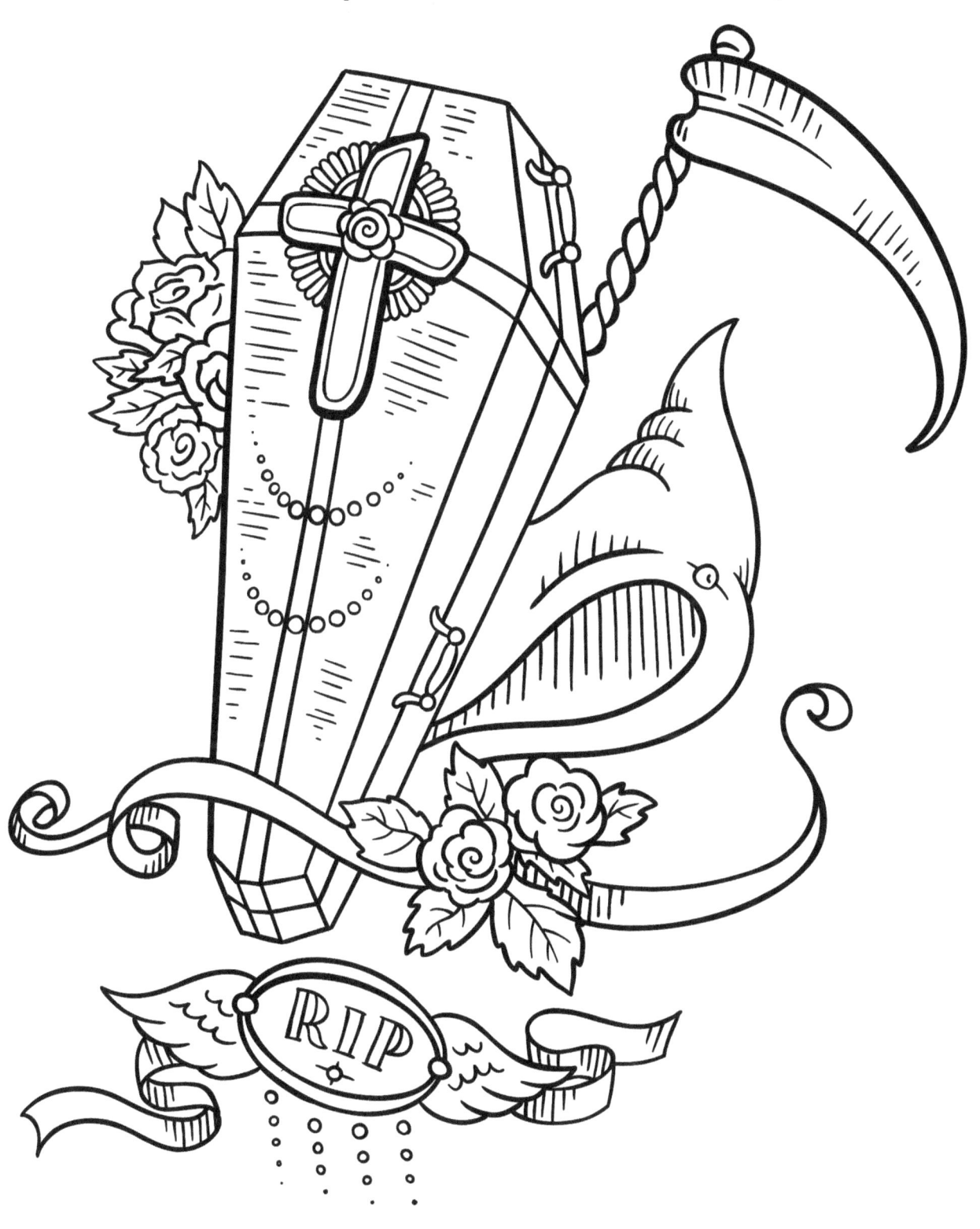

# About the Artist

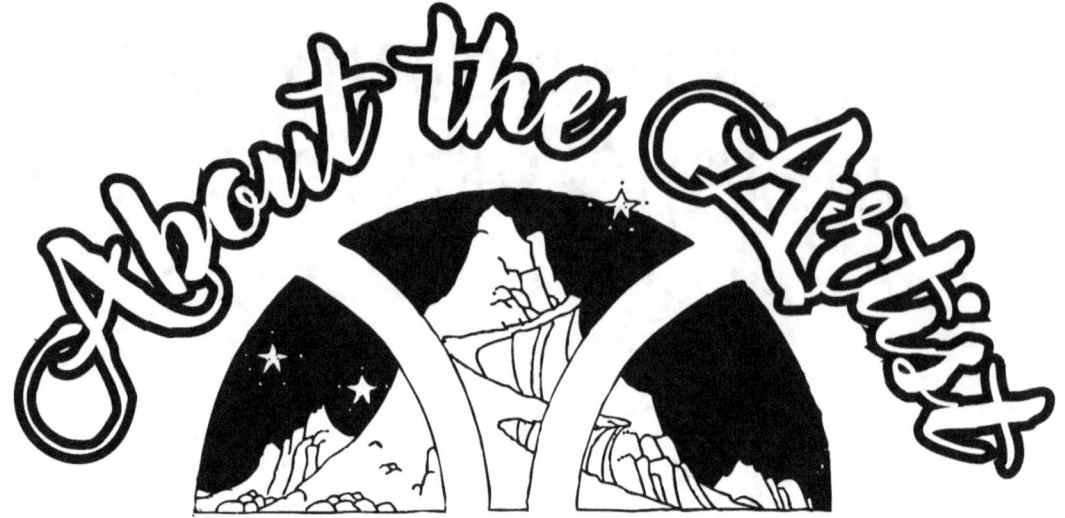

| Colored by | |
|---|---|
| On this day | |
| Notes | |

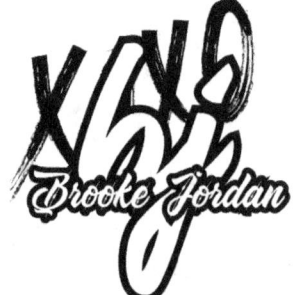

Amazon.com/author/bjos_Journals_etc

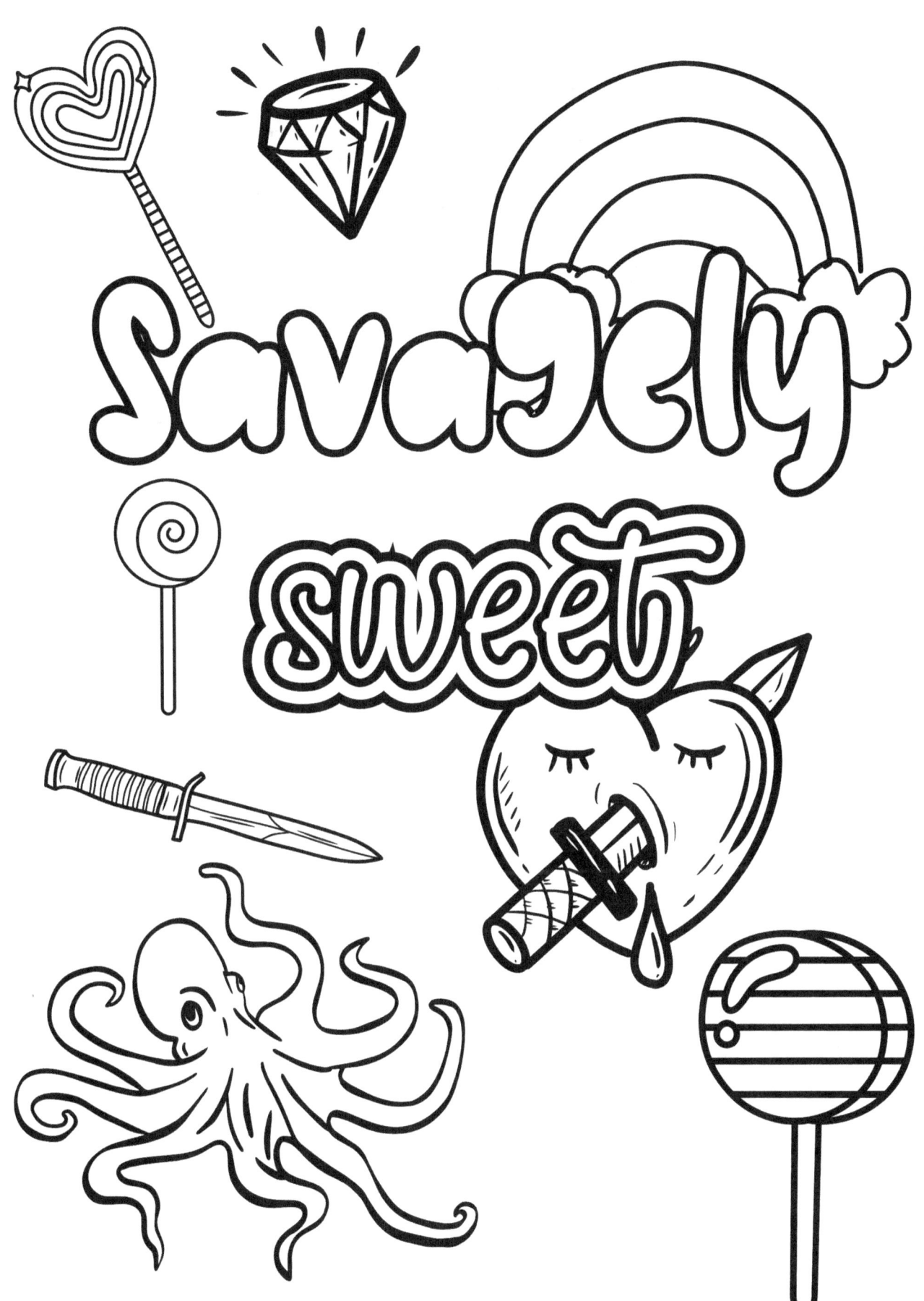

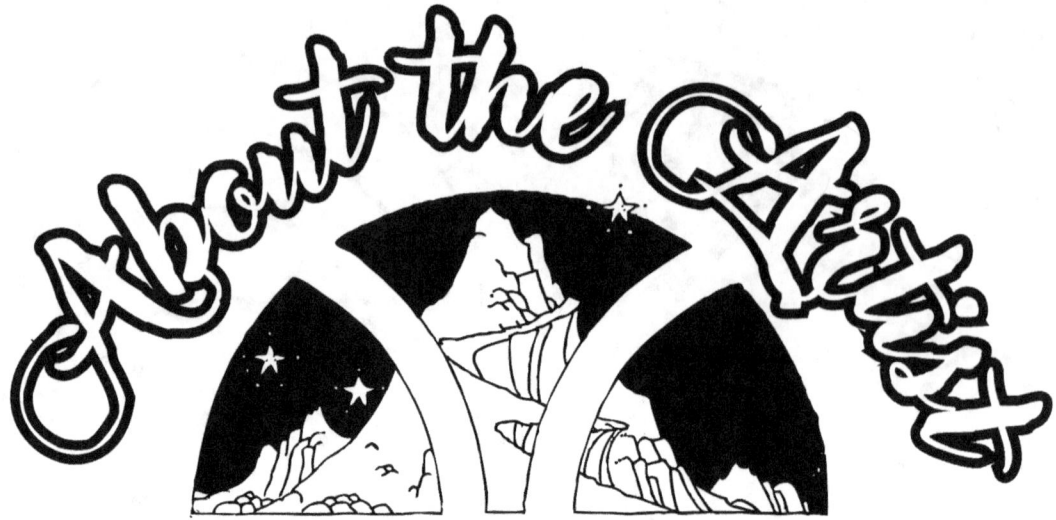

| Colored by | |
| On this day | |
| Notes | |

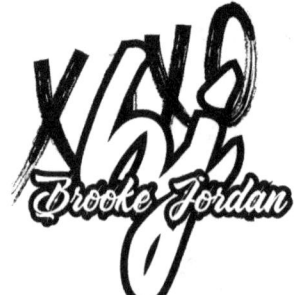

Brooke Jordan

Amazon.com/author/bjos_Journals_etc

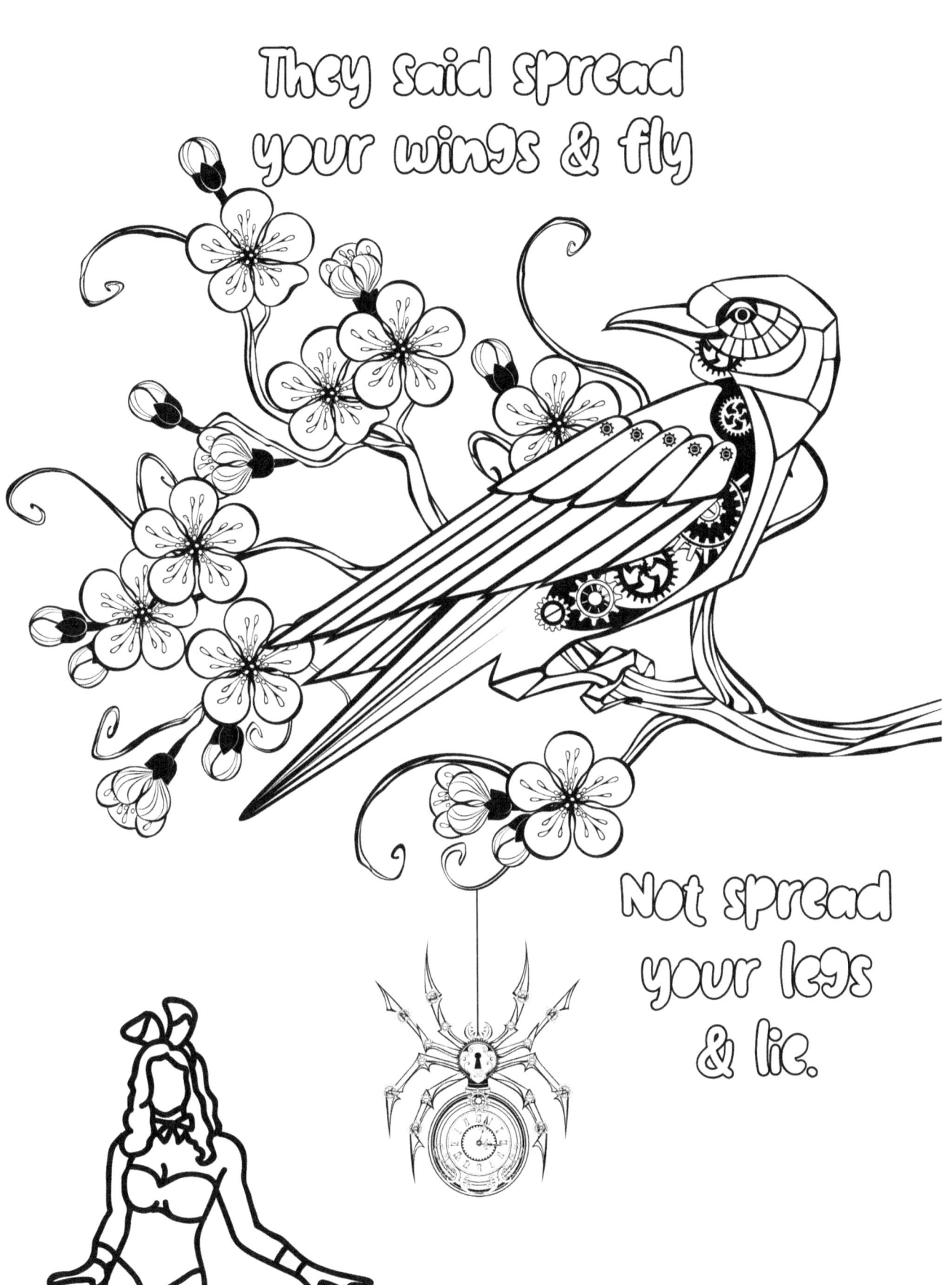

# About the Artist

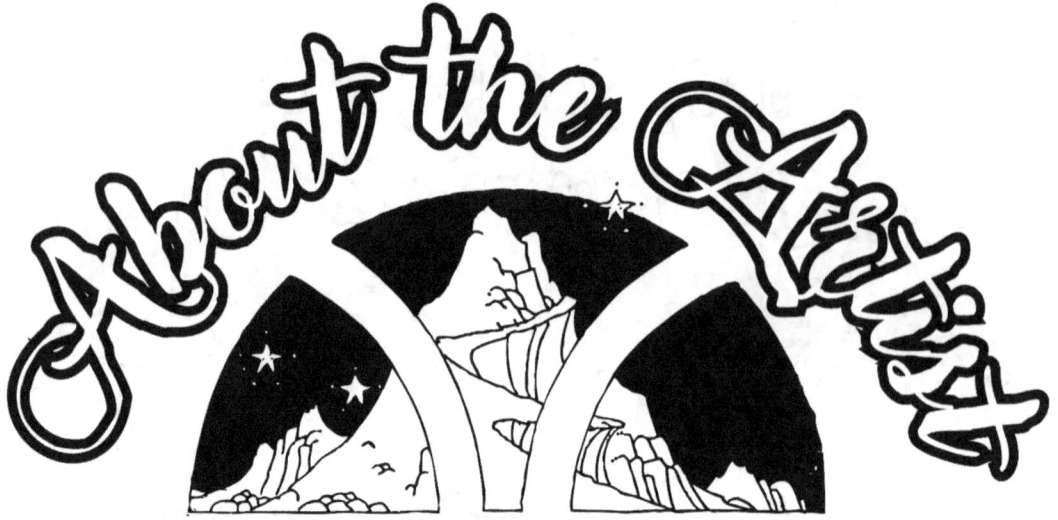

| Colored by | |
|---|---|
| On this day | |
| Notes | |
|  | |
|  | |
|  | |

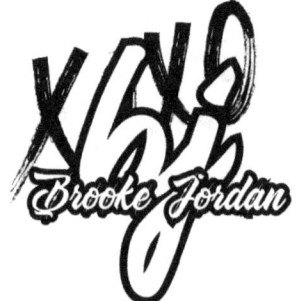

Amazon.com/author/bjos_Journals_etc

www.ingramcontent.com/pod-product-compliance
Lightning Source LLC
Chambersburg PA
CBHW062125220526
45471CB00010B/3880